"In a recent study on the effectiveness of Catholic Religious Education/Catechesis, two qualities of adult Catholics were mentioned: 1) committed to the proclamation of the gospel, and 2) reads/reflects on Scripture. *The Word of the Lord* speaks directly to these qualities. As a popular commentary this book flows out of the experience that McBrien has had with many different ministers of the Word and will assist adult Catholics and those who minister to them in their lifelong formation as disciples of Jesus."

Matthew J. Hayes
Executive Director
Office of Formation & Education
Louisville, Kentucky

"*The Word of the Lord: Reflections on the Sunday Readings* by Philip McBrien is a 'popular' lectionary commentary that offers a particular perspective on the weekly readings, raising interesting and important issues for the reader through summaries of the readings and reflective questions. This book may be useful in providing insight to lectors, guidance to discussion leaders of small faith-sharing or catechumenate groups, and as a resource for individuals seeking a simple introductory understanding of the biblical text."

Tricia Boyle
Faith Education Coordinator
Queen of Peace Catholic Church
Salem, Oregon

"This easy-to-use primer on the Sunday lections is a welcome resource for busy pastoral ministers who are ever alert for quality materials for various groups. It provides:

• A handy supplement to existing parish Bible study groups, especially in light of the well-crafted questions for reflection.

• An enticing sampler for parishioners who exhibit a beginning curiosity about the study of Scripture.

• A useful tool for thoughtful lectors as they prepare, individually or communally, to proclaim the Word in the assembly.

• A ready companion for individuals who have already incorporated Lectio Divina into their way of prayer.

• A well-constructed resource for ecumenical or convenanted communities who utilize the Common Lectionary for faith sharing."

Gretchen Hailer, RSHM
Consultant, Faith Formation

"I recommend *The Word of the Lord* to lectors, preachers, liturgy planners, Scripture study groups, Renew groups, and catechumens. The commentary on each reading is concise but packed with insights from the most current scriptural studies. Following each Sunday's commentaries are probing 'questions for reflection.' These take readers from the page to their own lived experience of church, nudging them toward an appreciation of the Scripture readings, both personally and communally."

Father George J. Wolf, Pastor
Queen of Peace Catholic Church
Salem, Oregon

The
Word
of the Lord

Reflections on the Sunday Readings

YEAR B

PHILIP J. McBRIEN

TWENTY-THIRD PUBLICATIONS

Mystic, CT 06355

Twenty-Third Publications
185 Willow Street
P.O. Box 180
Mystic, CT 06355
(860) 536-2611
800-321-0411

ISBN 0-89622-700-6
Library of Congress Catalog Card Number 95-60665
Printed in the U.S.A.

For Patrick and Brendan

Acknowledgments

Like its predecessor, this volume of *The Word of the Lord* results from a long-running conversation involving many people. At the outset I want to thank a few of those people who have conversed with me, and without whose help I would surely have remained deaf to God's word.

I owe much to the people and the pastoral staff of St. Thomas Aquinas parish in Indianapolis. I thank especially Julie Niec, Fr. Cliff Vogelsang, Patti Hair, Betty Bopp, Tom Agnew, Bill Bensch, Mary Henehan Yarger, Mary Carson, and Norma Carrigan. It was my privilege to work with all of these folks on various projects related to the lectionary. By now most have moved on to other venues, as I have done. Even so, their wisdom continues to inform me and guide me. They have inspired most of what is good in this book. On the other hand, if the book is lacking in any way, they are blameless.

As do many others, I owe an enormous debt to the late James B. Dunning. Fr. Jim's was a most eloquent and powerful voice inviting us to renew the church through conversation. He was mentor, big brother, and sparring partner to me, and more importantly, perhaps the most important *mystagogue* of our time. (To understand what this unusual term is, see the comments for Christmas, Mass during the day.) Jim's sudden death in the summer of 1995 leaves us all just a bit poorer.

The philosopher H.-G. Gadamer has taught that a conversation is a game, a to-and-fro similar to tennis or badminton. One partner states his or her case as well as possible, and the other responds in any of a million ways, all shaped by experience, tone of voice, mood, and myriad other factors. In any genuine conversation partners respond back and forth, until by mutual agreement they reach a point at which no more volleys are necessary. No one engages me in the game of conversation more energetically than does my wife, the Rev. Dana Morgan McBrien. We talk about many things, of course, but we also converse regularly about biblical texts, especially those of the lectionary. Sometimes we even argue about them. Can you imagine spouses arguing? A former teacher and a first-rate preacher, Dana insists on clarity in speech and in written work. We can all be grateful for her efforts. Without her attention, this would have been a lesser, weaker book.

CONTENTS

INTRODUCTION

We read these verses on the twenty-eighth Sunday in ordinary time:

> For living is the word of God and active and sharper than
> any two-edged sword, piercing all the way to the division
> between soul and spirit, between joint and marrow, and
> discerning the reflections and thoughts of the heart. And no
> creature is hidden before him, but all things are laid bare,
> open to the eyes of the word to whom we are responsible.
> (Hebrews 4:12–13, author's translation)

Most words are created by someone who speaks or writes, or signs. Nearly every word lies inert until it is read or heard or received in some manner. Almost every word is a group of letters, a collection of sounds, a part of a language, and a symbol that points beyond itself to name or to describe something. But the word of God is unlike all other words. Every word on the page you are reading at the moment, or on any other page for that matter, lives only when you bring it to life. The word of God lives and acts always, no matter what you do, no matter what I do. The word of God includes letters, sounds, whole languages, and symbols, but it is also much more than all of these things.

How does God's word act? The author of the letter to the Hebrews invites us to think of God's word as sharper than any two-edged sword, against which the body is defenseless. This word also has eyes. He (for the pronoun is masculine in verse 13) sees and knows and cuts open and lays bare all things. The word of God is the standard by whom everything is judged, and the irresistible sword by whom our hearts and souls and spirits are made plainly visible.

How do you respond to this portrayal of God's word? It certainly grabs my attention. It tells me that there is nothing that I can ever do or say, or think or feel, that God's word cannot see and measure. It assures me that with every breath I must try my best to do what God expects of me. It also insists that God's word is a living being, too big and too powerful to be encompassed in the pages of a book, or even in the pages of all the books that could ever be written (see John 21:25). The

Bible itself, therefore, cannot contain *all* of God's word. Finally, God's word confronts me with a choice, as it confronts you and everyone else. On the one hand I might try to ignore the irresistible and conduct myself in any manner that pleases me. On the other hand, I can listen, hear, understand, obey, and act responsibly. You decide: Which is the wiser choice?

In light of everything I have said thus far, why would I ever call this book *The Word of the Lord*? I present it as a hint of the many ways in which God's word confronts us through various texts. The subtitle describes the book's focus: It invites you to hear God's word through *Reflections on the Sunday Readings of Year B*, as the Roman Catholic church reckons things.

I want you to think of this book as an invitation. It tells you one author's ideas about the contents of some important parts of God's word. If I have done my job well, the book will also invite you to go beyond my reflections to listen more deeply to God's word in prayer and action, in continued Scripture study and reflection upon the accumulated wisdom of the church, as well as in the people and in the world around you.

How to Use This Book

To understand the scheme of the book, you ought to know a little about the Sunday readings. Roman Catholic worship is built upon formal prayers and rituals, and biblical texts arranged into a schedule, or calendar. The prayers and rituals have been bound into a book we call the sacramentary. We call our arrangement of biblical texts the lectionary. Together, these two parts comprise what is known as the *Missal*, the sourcebook for Mass.

The lectionary assigns readings, or *lections*, to each day of every week in every year. Sundays and solemnities and feasts make up a fraction of the lectionary. To make our lives a bit more complicated, the lectionary is constructed upon not one, but two cycles, or calendars. The more familiar calendar is known as the "temporal cycle." It schedules the various seasons of the year and the celebrations that define those seasons. Sundays and the principal celebrations are assigned readings according to a three-year rotation. Each year in the rotation is designated A, B, or C. Weekdays are assigned readings according to a two-year cycle.

The less familiar calendar is known as the "sanctoral cycle." As its name suggests, this is primarily a cycle of saints' feast days, but it also includes solemnities, such as the solemnity of the Immaculate Conception (December 8), and important feasts, such as the Transfiguration (August 6) and the Triumph of the Cross (September 14), and others. These occasions displace weekday readings whenever they occur, and the most important among them displace the readings assigned to Sundays in ordinary time. In 1997 and 2003, this will happen five times: The fourth Sunday in ordinary time will be displaced by the Presentation of the Lord, February 2; the solemnity of Saints Peter and Paul, Apostles, June 29, preempts the thirteenth Sunday in ordinary time; September 14 is the feast of the Triumph of the Cross, which takes the place of the twenty-fourth Sunday in ordinary time; All Souls day is celebrated on November 2, instead of the thirty-first Sunday in ordinary time; in place of the thirty-second Sunday in ordinary time, we commemorate the dedication of the church of St. John Lateran, the cathedral church of the bishop of Rome. None of these occasions affects the Sunday readings in 2000, but the Transfiguration replaces the eighteenth Sunday in ordinary time during that year.

This book deals with the readings of year B Sundays and celebrations according to the temporal cycle, and with only those other feasts that do alter the readings that are to be proclaimed at Sunday Masses. Otherwise it omits both the sanctoral cycle and weekday readings. In addition, different sets of readings are assigned to many events in the church year. On Christmas, for example, the church celebrates a Mass at midnight, a Mass at dawn, and another Mass during the day. On the third, fourth, and fifth Sundays of Lent, any parish may (and parishes celebrating the scrutinies must) proclaim year A readings instead of those of year B.

There are, therefore, some eighty-six chapters in this book. Each is identified by the Sunday, solemnity, or feast whose readings it considers, and each contains the following:

• A theme that I have found among the readings. It is one of many possible themes. If you do accept the book's invitation and study the texts in detail, you might find entirely different themes, or even none at all. I include mine to focus the reflections.

• Dates, in brackets. Here is an example: Since 1996-97 is year B in Catholic reckoning, that year's readings for the first Sunday of Advent are to be used on December 1, 1996.

Now, although Advent happens every year, the following year will be year C and the next, year A. On the first Sunday of Advent in those years the church uses different sets of readings. The year B readings for the first Sunday of Advent will be in effect on November 28, 1999, and again on December 1, 2002, and in every third year following. Each chapter names the next three dates upon which its readings are to be used.

•Complete references for, quotations from, and reflections on the day's first reading, second reading, and gospel. Only a reference is provided for the day's responsorial psalm, because unlike the other texts, which may be poetry, history, story, or other literary form, a psalm is always a prayer. Preferring not to comment on the psalms, instead I invite you to pray them. Read them (or even better sing them) aloud, and savor their beauty. By doing so, you will discover the prayer that has literally sustained the church through history.

•Questions. I intend these to be challenging. They ask for your careful consideration and for action. They clarify the various challenges borne in the texts they accompany. You will not answer them completely, on first, second, or even third encounter. I hope they spark your thinking and action, both now and in years to come.

What This Book Can Do

Now that you know how the book is structured, allow me to tell you what it can do:

•*Summarize readings and offer a particular perspective on them.* I assume that your experience of hearing readings proclaimed and explained at Mass leaves you hungry for more. You do not wish to commit to hard, technical Scripture study, but you are willing to invest a little time and energy to acquaint yourself with the readings in use at Mass. You seek simple explanations of these texts.

•*Provoke your reflection on issues raised by the readings.* The Bible is the most influential collection of literature ever produced. I do not wish to demean the holy books of people who are not Christians or Jews. Other scriptures, especially the Qu'ran, have also had enormous historical impact. It is fair to say, however, that biblical stories, images, teachings, and the conclusions drawn from them have shaped our world more profoundly than those of the Qu'ran have done. On a scale smaller than the historical, the Bible's many and varied texts bear the power to change lives. When we devote even a casual attention to biblical texts, as we are doing here, inevitably we raise important, sometimes vital, issues. This book directs your attention to some of those issues, especially with the questions that accompany each Sunday's, solemnity's, or feast's set of readings.

•*Help you to prepare to proclaim texts publicly.* If you are a lector or a teacher, or if you read aloud at any form of prayer service, you need at least a simple understanding of your text. Your job is not to analyze a text or to guide people into its intricacies. Homilists, exegetes, and other specialists do those things. Still you must present your text clearly, and with confidence. After all, your text is an important part of God's word. Although God's word lives and acts, the church literally depends on you to announce its texts. If you can know a little about what a text says, you have taken the first step toward proclaiming it with confidence. If, on the other hand, you have not the slightest notion of what is going on in a text, you cannot proclaim it well. Maybe you can use a simple guide, because many biblical texts are just plain difficult.

•*Focus a small group of Christian friends in discussion.* Since our origins, we Christians have been a talkative bunch. The first impulse of people who meet the risen Christ has always been to run out and announce the good news to someone else. Even those witnesses portrayed at the end of Mark's account of the gospel, too frightened to announce the resurrection to the apostles as instructed, eventually must have overcome their fears and blabbed (Mark 16:1–8, Easter Vigil, year B). Had they not, and had no one else told the story, there might be no Christian books in the Bible.

One way we encounter the risen Christ is by reading the Bible, even when texts do not speak of the resurrection. We can talk about what we find there. Like those blabby witnesses from Mark's account, we *must* talk about it. This book can provide a focus for your deep conversations with spouses and friends, and especially for faith-sharing group meetings.

•*Provide a simple guidebook for your parish catechumenate,* or for any interreligious gathering of friends wishing to sample the lectionary's riches. Although my primary audience is Christian, particularly Roman Catholic, there is no reason to exclude anyone from your conversations and faith-sharing. I have used many of the questions listed in this book in groups that included Jews, Muslims, Buddhists, agnostics, and atheists. The human issues raised in biblical texts are universal. Anyone who wishes to converse about them can and should be welcomed into conversation. A genuine welcome never downplays our Christian identity. It does, however, require that we listen sensitively and respectfully to other voices.

Keeping all these things in mind, you may find that this book works well as a discussion guide in your parish catechumenate. This is true because the lectionary does seem to have been arranged, in part, to invite all persons into continuing conversion. When catechumens are dismissed from liturgy to pray, to share faith, and to explore the readings, their catechists may find the questions presented here useful.

•*Provide a simple sourcebook for spiritual directors and the people they direct.* The lectionary's texts and the questions in the book invite reflection and action. They ask you to examine the choices you face, and to enact those options that are most compatible with the gospel. But this is precisely the invitation of most forms of spiritual direction.

•*Serve as a supplement for family religious education.* The lectionary has found ever-wider use in religious education in recent years, though not without some controversy. One advantage claimed by proponents is that since all generations of learners hear the same readings proclaimed at worship, it is a simple matter to focus intergeneration education programs on these texts. While children are not likely to read this book, it can help parents to explain the Sunday and feast day readings to their children. This book can help your family to read, to discuss, and to pray with the Sunday readings.

•*Invite you to read, study, and interpret biblical texts.* This book is an introduction. Consider it a taste, a sampler, even a teaser. Most of all, it wants to invite you to immerse yourself in history's most important collection of words. I hope you will hear this invitation.

What This Book Will Not Do

Having told you what my book can do, I must also make some disclaimers. It will not:

•*Take the place of your direct encounter with biblical texts.* Nothing should ever be allowed to stand in the way of your encounter with the magnificent literature in our Bible. It would be a cruel irony if a book called

The Word of the Lord prevented you from hearing or from even trying to hear the word of the Lord. If you only hear the word of McBrien, then something is wrong. If you must choose between one or the other, drop this book immediately and read your Bible or lectionary. After you have wrestled with the real thing, if you wish, come back to my book. It is almost certain that parts of the Bible will edify you and challenge you. Other parts are sure to confuse you or even infuriate you. Maybe I can help you to begin to sort some things out.

• *Provide you with the definitive interpretation of any biblical text, or pretend to make any such interpretation.* This book will not tell you what a text means, although I have made every effort to help you to see what each text says. There is a difference. Throughout this book I want to help you make sense of each text on a most simple level. It takes hard work to interpret texts responsibly (see Appendix), but I presume that you are reading this book because you have not yet decided to do hard interpretive work. I have done some of the necessary hard work to set a simple explanation of readings before you.

But isn't any statement of what a text says a form of interpretation? Isn't it a statement of what the text means? After all, we humans are meaning-making creatures. Constantly, relentlessly, we try to figure things out, to determine what things mean. Moreover, we interpret in ways shaped by our unique funds of experience.

Yes, when I describe for you what I see happening in a text, I give it a particular slant, an interpretation. This is unavoidable, and I will not pretend otherwise. But my point here concerns not what I have written but the manner in which I invite you to read it. Please read it as introduction only, and not as the last word, not as *the* meaning of any text.

• *Equip you with specialized tools for interpretation. The Word of the Lord* is a form of biblical commentary, more properly a lectionary commentary. But all commentaries are not alike, nor are all created equal.

A peek into any decent bookstore shows you shelf upon shelf of commentaries on the Bible. Lectionary commentaries are likely to appear only in catalogs and in specialized bookstores, but they are also quite numerous. Why are there so many? The quick answer is to say that the various commentaries address differing audiences, for specific purposes.

To understand this latter point more clearly, it helps to think of the various commentaries under two broad headings. "Scholarly" commentaries tend to be detailed, technical, usually hard to read, and often intimidating. That's the bad news. The good news is that the best scholarly works help us to open up texts, sometimes to find things we would almost certainly never see without their help. They equip us to dive deep into the waters of Scripture and to stay underwater for serious expeditions.

"Popular" commentaries, by contrast, tend to speak in general, non-technical terms. They try to be accessible and easy to read. Unlike scholarly works, however, they tend to close texts, rather than to open them. They help us to see only what can be seen fairly easily. They help us to stay afloat on the surface of the Bible, but they cannot sustain us under the surface for more than a few moments.

All of this is not to say that one kind of commentary is better than another. As I said earlier, there are differing audiences with specific needs and interests. It is legitimate that different kinds of commentaries address differing audiences.

This distinction will help you to understand what you can expect from this book. It is a "popular" commentary, in the technical sense in which I have used that word. I have used many of the best available scholarly works to produce it, and it is as reliable as I can make it, but it is not a work of scholarship. Many times I will tell you that "scholars say this" and "scholars say that." A work of scholarship would try to demonstrate why certain things have been said about any given text, while representing a wide range of viewpoints and marshalling evidence for selecting a particular view. Here I report on the fruits of scholarship in order to offer a simple explanation of what each text says. To go deeper, you must use a scholarly commentary, ideally in some form of conversation. And whatever do I mean by that? See the Appendix, which suggests a departure point for your continued study of Scripture.

•*Guide you through the mechanics of lector preparation.* I said earlier that a basic understanding of a text is your first step toward proclaiming it well. It is not the only step, however. *The Word of the Lord* equips you with an understanding of each text. It does not teach you about posture, elocution, tone, pace, or any of the other ingredients of excellent proclamation. Some books do try to assist you in these ways, but I think your better option is a sensitive coach. All the better if he or she is equipped with a video camera.

Listen for God's Word

The author of the letter to the Hebrews has insisted that God's word penetrates between joint and marrow, between soul and spirit, and discerns the reflections and thoughts of the heart. The word sees and evaluates all things. This volume of *The Word of the Lord* invites you beyond its own modest efforts to listen for God's word in the Scriptures, in your choices and actions, and in the world. It asks you to acquaint yourself with a huge and powerful Word whom we glimpse in the readings of year B.

FIRST SUNDAY OF ADVENT

We are clay

[December 1, 1996; November 28, 1999; December 1, 2002]

First Reading: Isaiah 63:16–17, 19; 64:2–7

You, Lord, are our father....

We begin this church year with fragments taken from a prayer of confession. The prayer is not the work of Isaiah, the great prophet who lived in Jerusalem seven centuries before the birth of Jesus Christ. Instead, it was created by an anonymous poet who composed the last chapters of this book, and who is frequently called "Third Isaiah." Speaking of the Jews' life in the promised land after their return from captivity, the prophet laments the people's continued hardness of heart: "Why do you let us wander?" The prayer calls for the return of the Lord, for the sake of the people who are still God's servants, however wayward they may have been. God never gives up on God's people.

Though intended for an audience very different from us, today's verses from the prayer speak on our behalf and set the tone for our Advent season: "Return for our sake, Lord God, our father. Tear the heavens and come to us, making the mountains tremble. It would be good if you found us doing right, but the odds are against it: We are angry, guilty, unclean. We do not pray as we ought, and yet...and yet...You are our father. We are clay, you are the potter. We are the work of your hands."

Responsorial Psalm 80:2–3, 15–16, 18–19

Second Reading: 1 Corinthians 1:3–9

Grace and peace from God our Father and the Lord Jesus Christ.

The tone of these verses could hardly contrast more with that of the first reading. At the beginning of what is considered his most important letter, Paul congratulates the Christians at Corinth for the favor that God has bestowed on them. Paul's own witness has been so confirmed that they lack no spiritual gift as they wait for Jesus' return. Christ will strengthen them to face whatever comes.

But like the first reading, this too speaks directly to us, as well as to its first audience. We have already been given everything we need to live in fellowship with one another and with Christ. Like the Jewish people newly restored to their homeland after years of captivity, we must place our whole lives in God's hands and allow ourselves to be shaped into useful vessels.

Gospel: Mark 13:33–37
Be constantly on the watch.

At the end of year A, on the feast of Christ the King, we proclaim Matthew's version of Jesus' final teaching before his passion. Today we encounter Mark's somewhat different version of the same event. "Stay awake!" says Jesus. "You do not know the appointed time. Your situation is just like that of servants placed in charge of the house while the master is away. You do not know when he might return, but you must be ready at all times. Do not let him find you asleep and unprepared."

Although Mark's older story differs from Matthew's, it is no less urgent. Here, since Advent is a season for preparation and renewal, it insists that we meet the responsibilities given to us.

Mark offers no specifics about those responsibilities, however, and perhaps that is the way things should be. Each of us has been given a distinct set of gifts and tasks, and the central task of discovering and doing what God expects of us. Together these three readings focus on our blessings, our shortcomings, and our challenge. We must look constantly for our God, who can burst into our lives at any time. That is our task during Advent. We must look, and prepare to receive the one who is coming. In the words of the first reading, we must allow the potter to shape us anew.

Questions for Reflection

•How do you wander? In what ways do you think you disappoint God, your father?

•How does a potter work with clay? What does this image suggest about God's work on you? How does God try to mold you and shape you?

•How has God blessed you? What does it take for you to place your whole life in God's hands?

•How do you prepare for an important appointment or visit? What do you feel? What do you do? How does your behavior differ from the routine? Compare and contrast your answers to these questions with your response to one more: How do you prepare for God?

Second Sunday of Advent

Prepare a path for the Lord

[December 8, 1996; December 5, 1999; December 8, 2002]

First Reading: Isaiah 40:1–5, 9–11

Here is your God!

The people of Judah have been uprooted from their homeland and held in captivity in Babylon. They have survived the onslaught of Assyria that had destroyed the northern kingdom and dispersed its ten tribes (2 Kings 17). One hundred and fifty years later their territory has been conquered, and most of the people have been deported to Babylon (2 Chronicles 36:15–21). Their links to place and political structure severed, they must either find a new source of identity or disappear from history, as their northern cousins have done.

The poet known as "Second Isaiah" encourages these people of Judah, from now on called "Jews," to find their identity anew in the God who has accompanied them throughout history. God comforts them and will not ask them to suffer any longer. A voice cries out: "Prepare the way of the Lord, make a highway in the desert. Mountains shall be leveled, and God's glory will be revealed. Go up to the mountaintop and announce to all the displaced people of Judah: Here is your God, who rules with strong arm and feeds the flock."

These words invite us, as well as the Jews of ancient times, to find our identity in God. Thanks to the enduring popularity of Handel's *Messiah*, we hear these words often during this season: "Here is your God!"

Responsorial Psalm: Psalm 85:9–10, 11–12, 13–14

Second Reading: 2 Peter 3:8–14

What we await are a new heaven and a new earth....

The author draws a contrast between our time frame and God's. What we may see as a delay in God's plan to end the world is instead God's expression of patience. God wants all to come to repentance. God is willing to wait.

But the day of the Lord will surely come, like a thief. It is essential that we conduct ourselves in holiness and devotion, anticipating that day. God will establish new heavens and a new earth, saturated with

God's justice. For our part, we cannot sit around idly. We must hasten that day, building justice and inviting all into holiness and devotion, keeping ourselves pure and at peace.

Gospel: Mark 1:1–8

Here begins the gospel of Jesus Christ....

The earliest of our four gospels, Mark's is also the shortest, and in most instances the most abrupt. An overwhelming body of evidence suggests that both Matthew and Luke used Mark as an outline. By contrast with the works of the other evangelists, Mark's gospel seems spare, unadorned, and right to the point. For nearly all of the current church year, we read from Mark's gospel.

The book begins by depicting the Baptizer obeying the command of today's first reading, to prepare a path for the Lord. From this point on, Mark wants us to see that everything is new. John draws great numbers of people to the Jordan, where he immerses them in a ritual bath peculiar to one Jewish sect of twenty centuries ago. He also preaches: "One is coming who is greater than I. I am not fit to untie his sandals. I baptize with water; He will baptize with the Holy Spirit."

There is something revolutionary going on here, and we must not allow its familiarity to obscure that fact. Like the uprooted people of Judah, we cannot find our identity in externals. Place of residence, political or church affiliation, even the public ritual of baptism cannot tell us who we are, cannot save us. What matters above all is our baptism in the Holy Spirit. But what is this? It is not an ecstatic experience, nor certainly an invitation for us to judge others. The rest of Mark's lean and muscular gospel offers strong clues. A person baptized in the Holy Spirit follows Jesus, by healing, consoling, and teaching all people the way to the cross.

Questions for Reflection

•Who are you? How do you define yourself? How many different names, roles, and characteristics describe you? Which of these is most important? Why?

•What does God seem to want you to do? How have you listened for God's expectations of you? When do you plan to do what God expects? How will you do these things?

•How does your baptism matter to you? According to Christian teaching, how is it supposed to matter? How much of a difference is there between the two answers? How will you try to bridge the difference? What sort of help do you need to build your bridge?

THIRD SUNDAY OF ADVENT

The ministry of the baptized

[December 15, 1996; December 12, 1999; December 15, 2002]

First Reading: Isaiah 61:1–2, 10–11

The spirit of the Lord God is upon me....

These verses have been extracted from a cycle of poems that comprises chapters 56–66 of our book of Isaiah. The cycle includes the works of an anonymous poet or group of poets writing during, or soon after, the Jewish people's exile in Babylon. The poems of "Third Isaiah" lack the literary brilliance of Isaiah of Jerusalem (chapters 1–39) or "Second Isaiah" (40–55). Even so, they introduce themes that are vital for us, especially expectation of the messiah and a fulfillment of hope in a new world to come.

The verses we read today portray the creation of a new Zion, or Jerusalem. The subject who will accomplish all the great things described is the messiah, the anointed of God. The spirit of God is upon the anointed one. The messiah will bring good news to the lowly, heal the brokenhearted, and proclaim liberty to captives and a year of favor for all. The messiah rejoices in the Lord, who has clothed the messiah in justice and salvation. As plants spring out of the earth, God will bring forth justice and praise before all the world.

We also proclaim these verses during celebrations of the sacraments of ordination and confirmation. This is no accident. The church uses these words to describe both ordained ministry and the ministry shared by all believers. After the example of the messiah, we are responsible for justice and salvation in the world.

Responsorial Psalm: Luke 1:46–48, 49–50, 53–54

Second Reading: 1 Thessalonians 5:16–24

May the God of peace make you perfect in holiness....

Paul concludes this very warm letter with advice and with his wishes for the church at Thessalonica. First, the advice: Rejoice always, pray and give thanks constantly. Do not stifle the spirit or despise prophecies. Test everything, keeping only what is good. Avoid evil in any of its appearances. Next, Paul's wishes: May God perfect you in holiness. May you be preserved when the Lord comes.

Gospel: John 1:6–8, 19–28

There was a man named John sent by God....

Today's verses amplify and provide a sort of commentary on last week's gospel. John the Baptizer is God's witness, testifying to the light that has entered the darkness of the world. When officials ask about his identity, John offers disclaimers: "I am not the messiah, nor Elijah, nor the prophet." He does claim, however, the role of the voice crying in the wilderness: "Make straight the way of the Lord." Under further questioning, John insists that he baptizes with water, but that one who is coming is greater than he.

Since the beginning, Christians have seen a connection between baptism and Christ's presence. Like John the Baptizer's relatively obscure Jewish bathing rituals in the Jordan, Christian baptism is a cleansing and a preparation. But more than these things, and far more importantly, it is also a celebration of the one who is present with us, right now, and forever.

When we speak of Christ's coming during Advent, we intend two things and imply a third. First, we commemorate the events of long ago, the birth of God as one of us, and his emergence through baptism into public life. Second, we anticipate the Lord's return, to end history. But we also know that Christ has been with us all along. Most of all, we prepare ourselves to greet Christ anew, and more deeply than ever before.

Questions for Reflection

•If the messiah brings justice and peace, how can Christians look honestly at our world and yet claim that the messiah has come? What evidence could suggest that the Lord's anointed has not yet arrived? What sense can it make for us to insist that the anointed has brought justice and peace to us?

•How does your daily conduct compare to what the second reading encourages: Rejoice; Pray; Give thanks; Do not stifle spirit or prophecy; Test everything; Keep what is good? What do you think you ought to do in response to this comparison?

•Why do Christians baptize? What does our baptism do for us? What does it accomplish on behalf of the church, and for the sake of the world?

•How do you live your ministry?

FOURTH SUNDAY OF ADVENT

House and throne

[December 22, 1996; December 19, 1999; December 22, 2002]

First Reading: 2 Samuel 7:1–5, 8–11, 16

...your throne shall stand firm forever.

These verses come from what may be called the court history of David, and they are among the first parts of the Bible committed to writing. They reflect a few of the many ways in which the people of ancient Israel understood the words "house" and "throne." Settled in his palace, the undisputed head of the twelve tribes, David declares his intent to build a house for the ark of God. Late at night, however, the Lord speaks to Nathan, reminding him of all the great things God has done for Israel, and of all the promises yet unfulfilled. Nathan must pose the rhetorical question to David: "Should you build a house for me?" In fact, God will establish a house for David, a house that will endure and reign forever.

In this text's wordplay, a house is more than a structure. It is a political dynasty, but more than that as well. Given the advantage of knowledge of history, we can see that David's "dynasty" will not survive his son Solomon. God intends to build a house that endures in memory and example, a symbol of the favor and the promise that sustain Israel through an often unkind history.

Responsorial Psalm: Psalm 89:2–3, 4–5, 27, 29

Second Reading: Romans 16:25–27

...may glory be given through Jesus Christ unto endless ages.

Paul concludes the letter to Rome with a doxology, or a hymn of praise. Its words may have been known to the letter's audience through frequent liturgical use. It is as though Paul spoke to us the familiar words: "Glory be to the Father and to the Son and to the Holy Spirit...."

The text is one very long sentence that tells us: "Let glory be given to God through Jesus Christ forever." But between the beginning and the end of this thought, the apostle summarizes some important teaching. God strengthens us in the gospel. The gospel reveals the mystery once hidden and now manifested through the prophets and to the Gentiles. May the Gentiles believe and obey. God alone is wise.

We too have been strengthened in the gospel and been privileged to witness the mystery. May glory be given to God, through Jesus Christ, and through us, his body.

Gospel: Luke 1:26–38

The Holy Spirit will come upon you....

Since ancient times the fourth Sunday of Advent has been a Marian feast. While Mark's brief and to-the-point account of the gospel anchors most of our readings during this year, it tells us nothing about Jesus' birth or childhood. For all the feasts surrounding Christmas, we must supplement Mark's account with texts borrowed from the other evangelists.

Here Luke describes the annunciation. The angel Gabriel greets Mary with words very familiar to Catholics: "Hail Mary! The Lord is with you. Blessed are you among women." Mary does not understand the greeting, so the angel continues: "You shall bear a son who will inherit the throne of David, and who will rule forever." Asking how this can be, Mary learns that the Holy Spirit will overshadow her, and that she will become pregnant with and give birth to the Son of God. The reading concludes as Mary accepts all these strange things proposed to her.

Mary is a most powerful symbol. Christians proclaim that David's throne has been made everlasting through her son, Jesus, that Jesus is the eternal king come forth from David's house. Just as important, Mary's encounter with the angel illustrates the receptivity that we call faith. Like Mary's, our journeys in faith begin in awe. Sooner or later they lead us to ask practical questions, which may include doubt but which always grow out of our particular circumstances. And sometimes our journeys take us to complete acceptance and gratitude.

Questions for Reflection

•Where does God live? How has your understanding of God's location changed as you have grown? What events fed these changes?

•How does Jesus Christ give glory to God? How does the church give glory to God? How do you do it? How do your actions, words, thoughts, and desires give glory to God?

•How and where did your faith journey begin? Where has it taken you? What questions have you asked? What questions have you failed to ask? How close do you seem to be to a place of acceptance and gratitude?

DECEMBER 25, CHRISTMAS, MASS AT MIDNIGHT

The prince of peace

First Reading: Isaiah 9:1–6

For a child is born to us....

Although these words express gratitude for Judah's liberation from the evil Assyrian empire, they also capture perfectly our sentiments on this day. A great light guides and shines upon the people who have walked in the dark. God has brought them great rejoicing, like that which accompanies the harvest. God has smashed the yoke, the pole, and the rod that have subjugated them. Now the clothes of battle may be burned for something useful, as fuel.

The one who is born to us is a royal child, whose name is Wonderful, Counselor, Almighty God, the Everlasting Father, the Prince of Peace. From David's throne he will govern a huge and peaceful kingdom through judgment and justice forever. Our God will do this!

History tells us that, in any literal sense, Isaiah's optimism was dashed quickly by continued royal habits of pettiness and short-sightedness. Judah never was able to live in peace or to elude external threat. When at last Assyria was overthrown, Judah was taken into exile by the conquering power, Babylon. Any promise of eternal peace and justice might have seemed remote, even a cruel hoax.

But God's promises do not go unfulfilled. The Jews have preserved Isaiah's words not only for their poetic beauty, but more importantly because they tell a deep truth. A child will be born to us who will illuminate the darkness that surrounds us. He will rule the world in peace and justice, forever. Christians insist that the child is already here. In many different guises Assyria still threatens us, and peace and justice remain hard to find. Even so, we proclaim God's promise fulfilled. The prince of peace is born, and we rejoice.

Responsorial Psalm: Psalm 96:1–2, 2–3, 11–12, 13

Second Reading: Titus 2:11–14

It was he who sacrificed himself for us....

This text reflects the paradox that dwells at the center of our faith. Christ has already redeemed the world, but this fact is not yet evident everywhere. Throughout history Christians have had to reckon with and live in this tension. We have been redeemed, but we do not yet see God face to face. Our sins are forgiven, yet we can and do fall into error. The prince of peace is here, but peace is hard to find. The author summarizes the benefits of God's grace, which offers salvation to all, and which trains us to live in preparation for the glory of God and our Savior Jesus Christ. Jesus has sacrificed himself for us, to save us and to cleanse us for himself. We proclaim a promise kept and, at the same time, a promise yet to be fulfilled. Our savior has come. Yet with our Jewish cousins we continue to wait for glory to come.

Gospel: Luke 2:1–4
...once they saw, they understood....
Like all of his people, Joseph must travel to his ancestral home, to be counted. Thus he arrives with Mary in Bethlehem, where Mary gives birth to her firstborn. She wraps him in swaddling clothes and lays him in a manger. Caesar's and God's purposes collide in an insignificant town in one of the empire's outlying provinces.

Today we are surrounded by the purposes of empire, either Caesar's or Assyria's, or someone else's. But the gospel announces God's purposes, which differ greatly from those of empire. To ensure that we do not overlook the significance of this birth, Luke tells us about shepherds watching their flock nearby in the night. God's angel appears to them as the glory of God bathes them in light, assuring them that they have nothing to fear. The good news is this, says the angel: "A savior has been born to you. He is the messiah and Lord. You will find an infant in a manger wrapped in swaddling clothes." Then a "multitude of the heavenly host" appears, shouting "Glory to God. Peace on earth to those whom God favors." A child is born to us, and we rejoice.

Questions for Reflection
•What empires try to bend us to their will today? What are their purposes? What do they want, and how do they pressure us to give them what they want? What are the dominant empires in the world? What forces cut across the boundaries of nations, peoples, and cultures to shape the world in which we live?

•What has God already accomplished through Jesus Christ? What promises remain yet unfulfilled?

•What are God's purposes? How do they differ from Caesar's, from Assyria's, from your own habits and expectations?

•How can we rejoice? How will you rejoice?

DECEMBER 25, CHRISTMAS, MASS DURING THE DAY

The word dwells among us

First Reading: Isaiah 52:7–10

All the ends of the earth will behold the salvation of our God.

These texts play a "mystagogical" role, teaching us the deeper significance of mysteries we already know, by experience, by heart.

Chapters 40–55 of the book with the prophet's name are often called "Second Isaiah." They begin with a message of consolation, then describe and interpret the sufferings of the Lord's servant. The final chapter portrays the Lord's banquet, at which all will fill themselves without cost, and with the promise that God's word will be fulfilled in the chosen people.

These verses describe the work of the servant, the one who brings glad tidings. We use them mystagogically here because they help us to dig ever more deeply into history's most celebrated birth. The servant's feet are beautiful upon the mountains. He announces peace, good news, salvation. He says to Jerusalem: "Your God is King! Pay attention! The watchmen shout for joy, because they can see God restoring Jerusalem. Sing, you who have been ruined, for God comforts and redeems the people. And all the world will know the salvation God has brought."

Responsorial Psalm: 98:1, 2–3, 3–4, 5–6

Second Reading: Hebrews 1:1–6

God...has spoken to us through his Son....

The author, who is not Paul, insists that the new revelation is superior to the old. The opening verses teach that until speaking through the Son, God had spoken in fragmentary and varied fashion. The Son is the agent through whom God has created all things, and the one whose word sustains all created things. Having cleansed us of our sins, the Son has been seated at the Father's right hand. He is superior to the angels.

Gospel: John 1:1–18

...enduring love came through Jesus Christ.

John's opening verses remind many observers of the chorus in a Greek drama. Before the drama begins, the chorus provides a context for, and a summary and interpretation of, what is to be presented. It is also intended to whet our appetites, to invite us into the drama. Often the chorus really is what we would call a chorus; that is, it is sung by several voices in unison, without costume or props.

We proclaim John's prologue-chorus. To appreciate its power, we might envision this text setting the stage for the liturgical drama that we enact through the seasons of the year. We already know the contours of the drama. We have heard them many times, and maybe we have tried to live them. Even so, we embark on this familiar journey once more, in order to enter more deeply into the mystery that is the Word dwelling among us.

"In the beginning...," chants the chorus, echoing the Bible's very first words. The Word was before all things, and all things came into being through him. The Word was with God and the Word was God. The Word brought light to a darkened and despairing world, and the darkness has never put it out. We should note here that neither has the light overcome the darkness. We live in between times, "already...but not yet." The savior has already come, but the final glory awaits.

John came to testify to the light. Maybe responding to first-century disputes, the prologue insists that John was not the light, but its witness. The light came into the world, and the world did not recognize him. Whoever did accept him has become a child of God. The Word became flesh and pitched his tent among us; we have seen his glory, the glory of a Son filled with enduring love. While the law was a gift through Moses, enduring love came through Jesus Christ. Jesus the Son has revealed God to us. That is a mystagogical way of thinking about Christmas, a way that deepens our understanding of the familiar that is also mysterious.

Questions

•How has Jesus filled the role of God's servant? In what specific ways has Jesus served God in your life? Who bears the role of servant now? How do you contribute to this role?

•Why do the epistle and gospel texts both insist that Jesus has played a big part in the creation and ongoing life of the world?

•In what specific ways does the chorus-prologue of John's gospel invite you this year? How have you responded to the drama of the gospel in the past? How will you respond this time around? What do you need? Whom will you ask for help, and how?

•In what ways are we responsible to the world?

HOLY FAMILY, SUNDAY IN THE OCTAVE OF CHRISTMAS

Family and community

[December 29, 1996; December 26, 1999; December 29, 2002]

First Reading: Sirach 3:2–6, 12–14

...kindness to a parent will not be forgotten,...it will take lasting root.

Deep in our hearts, most of us know what good family relationships are supposed to be. These verses describe them with great clarity, praising obedience, expounding on the fourth of the ten commandments. God has set father and mother in positions of honor and authority over their children. To honor one's parents is to be blessed with children, to pray effectively, to live a long life, to obey the Lord. One who lives by the fourth commandment will reap all manner of blessings as a reward for his or her obedience.

These words typify the work of the author, the Egyptian teacher Yeshua ben Sira, also known as Sirach. Originally written in Greek and later omitted from Jewish and Protestant Bibles, Sirach's observations on the ways of the world seek to demonstrate the superior wisdom of the Jewish way of life. We act wisely when we maintain and revere good relationships with our parents.

Responsorial Psalm: Psalm 128:1–2, 3, 4–5

Second Reading: Colossians 3:12–21

Christ's peace must reign in your hearts.

How are Christians supposed to act? This reading lists the major motives of persons who live in Christian communities, especially in Christian families. The author tells the members of the church at Colossae that because they are God's chosen ones, they face special obligations. They must bear with one another and forgive one another as God has forgiven them.

The last paragraph of this text sounds a note so jarring that it could ruin the impact of the entire passage for many people today. For others, the language poses no problem at all. Wives are told to be submissive to their husbands. Some people find this language offensive and antiquated. Others find it a precise description of a divinely ordained way of organizing human affairs. This latter position assumes naively that an imperative given to one culture should be imposed upon another, with no attention to nuance or cultural differences. Christian marriages, sacraments of God's presence among us, have neither room nor time for the sort of domination or enslavement connoted by "submission."

The virtues and motives listed earlier suggest a clue by which we might understand this paragraph. If we enact the habits that build Christian community, "submission" assumes a secondary importance. More important are mercy, kindness, humility, meekness, patience, forbearance, forgiveness, and most of all, love. In other words, each of us must be submissive to the greater good of community and mutual love.

Gospel: Luke 2:22–40

This child is destined to be the downfall and rise of many in Israel....
Joseph and Mary go to the temple in Jerusalem for purification according to the law of Moses (see Leviticus 12:2–8). There they meet Simeon, possessed of the Holy Spirit, who sees in the child something extraordinary, a savior, a light, a sign, the downfall and rise of many. While observing the laws of his people, Jesus' family learns that he will shake up the order of things in ways that they cannot yet understand.

Anna, described here as prophetess and widow, observes Simeon's identification of the child, and talks about Jesus to everyone seeking Jerusalem's liberation. After accomplishing all that the law requires, Joseph and Mary return to Nazareth. Jesus grows in size and strength and wisdom, with the grace of God upon him.

Questions for Reflection

•How good is your relationship with your parents? What about the relationships with your children? What improvements can you make? How will you make these improvements?

•How do your motives and habits compare to the second reading's list of virtues: mercy, kindness, humility, meekness, patience, forbearance, forgiveness, and love? What must you do to wear love as your outermost garment?

•In which Christian communities do you participate? The more obvious ones are family and parish, but what are your other communities? How well does each of these communities embody the second reading's virtues?

•How is Jesus the rise of many? How is he the downfall of many? How well do you like these words? How can you make sense of them?

MARY, MOTHER OF GOD, JANUARY 1

Abba!

First Reading: Numbers 6:22–27

The Lord bless you and keep you!

According to Hebrew tradition, this is a most ancient and solemn blessing, grounded in the unimpeachable authority of Moses. The Lord has told Moses to teach the priests of Israel, Aaron and his descendants, that they must bless Israel in this manner:

May the Lord bless you and keep you!

May the Lord shine the divine face upon you and be gracious to you!

May the Lord look upon you kindly and give you peace!

In each *stich*, or line, a second statement defines and clarifies the first. Thus to wish for God's blessing is also to desire God's protection. God's shining face upon us is related to graciousness, probably best understood as hospitality. And God's kind look upon us is virtually the same thing as the gift of peace.

This text is positioned dramatically. As we read it, we invite God's protection, graciousness, and peace in all our endeavors through the year ahead.

Responsorial Psalm: Psalm 67:2–3, 5, 6, 8

Second Reading: Galatians 4:4–7

You are no longer a slave....

Continuing through the Christmas season to reflect upon mysteries that seem familiar to us, we read texts mystagogically. In these verses Paul describes and interprets the birth of God's Son. Heirs who are underage are not really treated as heirs: They must be supervised. But now God's promise has been kept, in the person of God's Son. The Son has been born under the law, in order to free its subjects. At the appropriate time, the Son has made it possible for all to be God's adopted children. The proof is observable: People who were once as slaves can now cry out *Abba* ("Daddy!"), prompted by the Spirit.

If this last point were Paul's major one, it could cause real trouble. After all, anyone saying the right words could claim divine justification. In fact, some people do act this way. But through this entire letter

Paul also challenges the audience to live transformed lives worthy of God's faith in us.

Gospel: Luke 2:16–21

Mary treasured all these things and reflected on them in her heart.

Here is another small scene that sharpens our focus on the mystery that is God born a child. It is framed and enlarged by the arrival, departure, and return of shepherds. Having seen an angel (2:9–13) they rush to Bethlehem, where they find Mary and Joseph, and the baby lying in the manger. They understand what was told to them, and they depart to announce what they have seen and heard. Their activity is a simple and incomplete form of evangelization. It is incomplete because they cannot know anything at this point about Christ's passion and resurrection. They have not yet witnessed the gospel. They can tell what they do know, however, which is that a messenger (angel) has taught them that this child is the long-awaited messiah, the one who will deliver Israel from bondage. And they can return to the manger to describe the astonishment that has greeted their news. But despite the words of the text, they cannot really understand, not as later generations can do.

We should contrast their actions with those of Mary. Mary knows no more about the trajectory of Jesus' life than do the shepherds, but she has been privileged with a deeper kind of knowledge. Something extra has been revealed to her. The child is God's Son. She treasures this secret and all these other things, and reflects upon them in her heart.

Like the shepherds, we must respond to the great gift of Christmas. Like Mary, we must also treasure all that has been revealed to us, especially if it is most familiar. Lacking this deeper awareness, our words and actions might astonish, but they cannot announce the gospel.

Questions for Reflection

• How does God bless you? How does God shine the divine face on you? In what kind ways does God look upon you?

• How do you address God? How often do you use a comfortable, familiar term like "Daddy"? What is keeping you from speaking to God in this way more often?

• What do you treasure and reflect upon in your heart?

• How do you announce the good news? How do people respond to you?

• How will you celebrate God in our world, as you embark on this new year?

EPIPHANY

God's self-disclosure

[January 5, 1997; January 2, 2000; January 5, 2003]

First Reading: Isaiah 60:1–6

...upon you the Lord shines.

It is said that a light as small as a match can be seen at night from a distance of many miles. The author of this text wrote when only natural light, and relatively tiny pinpoints of human-made fire, could allow people to see. In the darkness that covers the earth, Jerusalem is illuminated in the glory of the Lord. The divine light shall guide nations and their kings, and indeed all the peoples of the earth. From everywhere people will come, bearing gifts, guided by the light that is the Lord's glory.

The anonymous poet often called "Third Isaiah" speaks to a generation returned from exile. This text invites us to stand beside the chosen people, newly restored to their homeland, to look into the darkness from a brilliantly lit place. See, says the prophet, all the nations of the earth walk by your light, and they come to you.

For us, the most interesting gifts are named in the final verse: Travelers from Sheba shall bear gold and frankincense. Today's gospel adds to these myrrh, a burial spice. Christians insist that Jesus has taken on the blessings and the responsibilities of the chosen people. He has done this by dying and rising. He has endowed his followers with his glory and his responsibilities.

Responsorial Psalm: Psalm 72:1–2, 7–8, 10–11, 12–13

Second Reading: Ephesians 3:2–3, 5–6

...the Gentiles are now co-heirs....

According to the author, in Christ Jesus the Gentiles are now co-heirs with the Jews, members of the same body and sharers of the same promise given to Abraham and his descendants. There is a double irony here. First, the Christian claim to Israel's promise is outrageous, from a Jewish perspective. How would you like it if a stranger tried to claim your identity? How would you feel if you caught someone else wearing your clothes, mimicking your speech, affecting your mannerisms, claiming even your family?

Second, the author of this letter, who is not Paul, nonetheless writes in Paul's name. Pseudonymous writing is common in ancient literature, as today's first reading also illustrates. This author probably never had a second thought about writing under Paul's identity, or about Christians claiming the inheritance of the Jews. But on this festival of light piercing the darkness we must think twice. If we are to be co-heirs, let us not forget the illuminated audience of the first reading, heirs to God's promises when we were still pagans.

Gospel: Matthew 2:1–12
They prostrated themselves and did him homage.

The Epiphany is the earliest feast associated with the birth of Christ to be celebrated by the church. Only in later years did the church pay attention to Christmas day. Epiphany is also the principal Christmas feast in much of the world today. We tend to overlook it in our fast-paced society. We must slow down and take a good look at this event whose name means God's self-revelation.

In the first reading, God is revealed in the people of Israel. Here, pagan wise men, who represent all the nations of the world, see God in the face of the infant under the light of a star. They have followed a star to the stable. First dropping in on Herod, eventually they find their way to Bethlehem, where they present to the infant Jesus gifts of gold, frankincense, and myrrh.

The Epiphany illustrates perfectly the revolutionary nature of our faith. With the rest of the world, we long for images of royalty and the trappings of privilege. Here, these things are stood on their heads. Visitors bearing fabulous wealth brave untold miles and a jealous king to gaze into the face of a baby. This baby is the light who guides our world through the dark. He bathes us in the brilliant light that is God's glory, while also placing upon us serious ethical and social responsibilities. Like our cousins the Jews, we are examples for the rest of the world. Our king is born, and our star is rising. Let us live up to our calling.

Questions for Reflection
• How has God fulfilled promises made to you? How has God more generally fulfilled promises made to God's people? In turn, what are some of your responsibilities? How will you meet them?

• How do you think and act toward people of other faiths in general, and toward the Jewish people in particular? How do these readings challenge you? How do they affirm you?

• What led pagan visitors to the stable? How do you reveal God's glory to others? How might you begin to do this, if you do not already do so?

THE BAPTISM OF THE LORD

Called to bring justice

[January 12, 1997; January 9, 2000; January 12, 2003]

First Reading: Isaiah 42:1–4, 6–7

Here is my servant, whom I uphold....

This is the first of the four "servant songs," which are the work of the mysterious prophet known as "Second Isaiah." The Lord's voice insists that justice is the core of the servant's mission. The servant will open the eyes of the blind, bring out prisoners from confinement, and lead into light those who live in darkness. The servant is the one upon whom God has placed the divine spirit, the one who will bring justice to the nations. The servant shall not cry out in the street or break a bruised reed or quench a smoldering wick, until justice is established throughout the earth. God has called the servant for the victory of justice, taken the servant by the hand, formed the servant as a covenant, a light for all peoples.

From the beginning, the identity of the servant has been ambiguous. Was the servant a contemporary of the exiled Jews? Was the servant a "messiah" (anointed one) yet to come? Was the servant the Jewish people themselves? All these answers are possible. But one thing remains clear: The servant brings justice to the earth. We recognize the servant through his or her acts of justice, in the blind receiving sight, in the release of captives, and in light given to those in the dark.

Responsorial Psalm: Psalm 29:1–2, 3–4, 3, 9–10

Second Reading: Acts of the Apostles 10:34–38

...God anointed him with the Holy Spirit and power.

Luke's account of church origins includes several early homilies. Here he describes Peter preaching to a group assembled at the home of a Roman centurion. This Cornelius has just seen a vision of a man in dazzling robes, a reminder of what the women witnessed at Jesus' empty tomb (Luke 24:4; Acts 10:30ff.). The vision has told Cornelius to cross all cultural boundaries and to invite Simon Peter to his house. For his part, Peter has also had a vision (10:9–16) that insists that God alone decides what or who is clean.

Peter preaches and the whole household is baptized. Peter explains this action to his astonished companions by insisting that the Holy

Spirit has descended upon these Gentiles, as the Spirit had filled the Twelve on Pentecost day.

These verses give us the first half of Peter's homily. He has discovered that God shows no partiality. Anyone who fears God and acts uprightly is acceptable to God. Speaking to his audience as foreigners, Peter knows that they have heard about Jesus of Nazareth, but still he begins a summary of the gospel. Intentionally incomplete, this text reminds us of the drama, the risks, and the demands, of Christian baptism.

Gospel: Mark 1:7–11

You are my beloved Son. On you my favor rests.

Scholars today think that Mark is the oldest account of the gospel, written between 55 and 70. In general, Mark's account is the most spare, the most abrupt of the four. It begins with a description and interpretation of the Baptizer, whose appearance reminds people of Elijah.

These verses describe the beginning of Jesus' public ministry. John announces the one more powerful than himself, who will baptize in the Holy Spirit. Jesus appears and John baptizes him. When he emerges from the water, Jesus sees the sky split in two and the Spirit descending on him. And a voice names him: "My beloved Son. My favor rests on you." Lacking the infancy stories and the genealogies provided by other evangelists, Mark portrays Jesus coming from out of nowhere, passing through his baptism and into the public eye.

Our baptism too is a passage. It marks our initiation into the Christian community, with all the responsibilities that Christ has given us. In our baptisms, like Jesus, and like the servant in Isaiah 42, we are called to bring justice to the nations.

Questions for Reflection

•What is justice? How does God's servant bring justice to the earth? What demands does the servant's mission of justice place upon you? Who is the servant, anyway?

•How well do you imitate God, who shows no partiality? How must you improve?

•Why was Jesus baptized? Why were you baptized (or: Why do you look forward to your baptism?) What difference does your baptism make to you, to your family, to your friends, to your neighborhood, to all the circles in which you travel, to the world?

•What can you do to live your baptism more effectively than you already do?

ASH WEDNESDAY

Rend your hearts

[February 12, 1997; March 8, 2000; February 12, 2003]

First Reading: Joel 2:12–18

Rend your hearts, not your garments....

In the first centuries, before there was a universal calendar and even before there was a Bible as we know it, local churches were the only means through which the gospel could be made known to the world. When pagans and some Jews expressed their desire to become Christians, the churches had to ask them some hard questions: Why do you want to do this? What is going on inside you, underneath your wish to be included in the church? How has God acted in your life, and how have you responded? And are you really ready to leave behind your old life and to be made anew in the image of the crucified one? As the church developed and grew, these questions took on new forms, but they stayed with us. They were and remain the foundation of the season we call Lent.

We begin with an invitation that gets down to the basics. "Return to me with your whole heart," says the Lord, "in fasting, weeping, and mourning. Rend your hearts, not your garments. Return to your God who is merciful and gracious."

The imagery tells us that externals matter not at all. If we presume to tear only our garments or other external things, we accomplish nothing. Our words mean little apart from action motivated by a deep desire to walk in Christ's footsteps to the cross.

Our lives are more complex, and more fragile, than we imagine. We are just like Joel's first audience, whose only real security rested in God, and who knew this to be true. Yet like them, we too easily place our hopes in other things. In fact, if not in name, we drift away from God, taking our hopes to the altars of lesser, inadequate gods. Return to the Lord who is gracious and merciful, who is kind and who forgives. Rend your hearts, not your garments.

Responsorial Psalm: Psalm 51:3–4, 5–6, 12–13, 14, 17

Second Reading: 2 Corinthians 5:20–6:2

Now is the day of salvation!

Even though today we belong to a worldwide and highly structured church, like our ancestors we are still the primary expression of the gospel in the world. Laws and catechisms and even the Scriptures are part of our life, part of us. But nothing can take the place of our believable witness to the gospel. We are ambassadors for Christ. What we do reflects upon God. Because the stakes are so high, Paul speaks passionately: "I beg you, in Christ's name, be reconciled to God!"

Gospel: Matthew 6:1–6, 16–18
...your Father who sees in secret will repay you.

Here, as throughout the sermon on the mount, Jesus desires good motives even as he disdains appearances. He seems to dismiss as hypocrisy any good act that draws attention. "Do not let others see your religious acts," he says. "Assist the poor quietly and without fanfare. Keep secret the merciful actions you perform. Do not pray like hypocrites, in public. Instead, go to your room and pray in private. Neither should you fast as hypocrites do. Instead, groom your hair and wash your face, so that only your Father can see."

This text accompanies the distribution of ashes, through which we mark ourselves as Christians embarking upon Lent. Together, these three readings put each one of us on the spot. We are invited to return. We are challenged to live up to the grace that has been given to us. And we are told to avoid the appearance of hypocrisy, even as we mark ourselves.

Questions for Reflection
•Why do you want to be a Christian? Even if you have been one for years, the question is still essential. What is going on inside you, underneath your wish to be included in the church? How has God acted in your life, and how have you responded?

•In what ways are you responsible to others? How are you and other Christians responsible to the world? How will you accept and meet your responsibilities during this season?

•Why do we mark ourselves with ashes, right after reading Jesus' caution against appearances? How can we justify this practice?

•How do you pray? What do you hope to accomplish when you fast, assist the poor, and give mercy? Why do you do these things? Who can see you doing them?

•What changes must you make to rend your heart, not your garments?

First Sunday of Lent

Baptism

[February 16, 1997; March 12, 2000; February 16, 2003]

First Reading: Genesis 9:8–15

I am now establishing my covenant with you....

Floods that inundated the Middle East at the dawn of history are remembered in stories produced by several ancient cultures. The Hebrew version, which is the story of Noah, is the most familiar to us. Today we read the conclusion of the biblical story, in which God covenants with Noah, with Noah's descendants, and with every living creature rescued in the ark. The covenant is a promise: God will never again destroy the earth by flood. The rainbow that appears in the sky after a storm is the sign of the covenant between God and the earth.

In language and in tone, the Hebrew flood story is a story of creation, or more precisely, of a renewed creation. Our ancestors viewed the flood as God's way of starting over. Through cataclysmic waters God cleansed the earth, destroying what was bad and preserving the good. The church has set this story at the beginning of our annual retreat that culminates in baptisms at Easter. Among the many things we can see in this text, we ought to pay special attention to the flood as an ancient prototype for Christian baptism, and a lens through which we may understand our baptism more deeply.

The covenant expressed in the rainbow invites us to receive all of God's gorgeous creation as gift and sign of God's love for us. With the other readings, this text invites Christians into the cleansing and re-creation called Lent. Most of us will renew our baptisms through lenten disciplines. God invites us again to be cleansed of what is bad, so that the good may survive and flourish.

Responsorial Psalm: Psalm 25: 4–5, 6–7, 8–9

Second Reading: 1 Peter 3:18–22

You are now saved by a baptismal bath....

This letter ascribed to Peter is a collection of early baptismal homilies, many of which originated after Peter's death. Christian baptism is not the same as, and is much more than, the ritual cleansings celebrated by

John the Baptizer. Baptism is much more than a universal cleansing or the particular removal of a personal stain, although it is certainly a bath. These verses find an exact correspondence between baptism and ark. Like the rainbow that has revealed the significance of the flood, baptism is our pledge that we will live with irreproachable conscience through the resurrection of Jesus Christ.

Gospel: Mark 1:12–15
Reform your lives and believe in the good news!

After John's arrest, Jesus appears in Galilee proclaiming the good news with words that summarize our task during this season: This is the time of fulfillment. The reign of God is at hand! Reform your lives, believe in the good news.

At first glance, this text seems to view baptism from an angle that differs from that of the first two readings, in which the waters conclude a long process of cleansing. In Mark's account, the test occurs after the waters have done their work, both in the wilderness for forty days, and extended over the next years in Jesus' public career. Moreover, the test of all tests is the cross. But what is of real interest here is not the order in which events are narrated, but the new significance with which Jesus has endowed the waters. Christian baptism is a reminder of creation renewed and a cleansing bath. It is also above all our participation in Christ's life and work. It is our time in the desert, facing the tempter head-on. It is the great healings and miracles and teaching of our Master, and the more modest but no less important healing and miracles and teachings that we enact in his name. It is our immersion in the cross, in which we say "No" to death and every dead end that could trap us, if we allowed it to do so.

Questions for Reflection
• What promises has God made to you? Along with baptism, rainbow, and cross, what signs remind you of God's promises?

• What do you think God expects of you?

• What are your baptismal promises? If promises were made on your behalf years ago, which do you now accept as your own? Which promises are you not yet ready to fulfill? Who or what can help you to make good on these additional promises?

• What difference does it make to us that Jesus has endured temptation? How does his example instruct you? How does he challenge you?

Second Sunday of Lent

The Son

[February 23, 1997; March 19, 2000; February 23, 2003]

First Reading: Genesis 22:1–2, 9, 10–13, 15–18
Do not lay your hand on the boy.

These verses sketch one of the Bible's most terrifying stories, the whole of which we read at the Easter Vigil. In what seems to be a test of Abraham's faith, God appears to demand that he sacrifice his only son, Isaac. The demand is cruel, and seems absurd in light of God's repeated promise that Abraham will be father to countless descendants (Genesis 12:2; 12:17; 15:5; 17:4ff.; 18:18; 21:18). Even so, Abraham takes Isaac to Moriah, prepares the altar, and lays the boy on it. At the last possible moment a messenger from God halts the downward arc of Abraham's knife and assures Abraham that because of his obedience God will bless him with countless descendants.

For millennia, readers have tried all manner of strategies for coping with the difficulties in this story. Because chapter 22 is known to be a late addition to Genesis, some say that it simply does not belong there. Others insist that from the start the once-pagan Abraham has misunderstood God's intention. Others read the story as an allegory for Hebrew history. While these and other interpretations may contain pieces of the truth, we cannot ignore the story's awful demands. Against all reason, Abraham is asked to sacrifice the only son born to him and his wife in their old age. Abraham's response is simple and haunting: "I am ready."

Responsorial Psalm: Psalm 116:10, 15, 16–17, 18–19

Second Reading: Romans 8:31–34
If God is for us, who can be against?

The epistle draws a contrast with the first reading. The entire text consists of questions: Can God who did not spare God's own son not grant us all things? Who will accuse the chosen ones? Will God accuse? Will Jesus condemn? For Paul, Christ's sacrifice has rendered these and all such questions absurd. God's own power has been bestowed upon us. Nothing else matters.

34

Gospel: Mark 9:2–10

This is my Son, my beloved. Listen to him.

The readings on the second Sunday of Lent always tell of both Abraham and the transfiguration of Jesus. Readings in year A and year C stress different facets, but these texts focus our attention on the Son sacrificed, as well as on the son nearly sacrificed.

Jesus takes Peter, James, and John to the top of a mountain where before their eyes he is transfigured, that is, changed in form and appearance. His clothes become dazzling white, and Elijah and Moses converse with him. Peter wishes to build booths, or tents, for Jesus and these two Hebrew saints, but this does not happen. Instead a cloud overshadows all, and a voice from the cloud teaches: "This is my beloved Son. Listen to him." And looking around, Peter, James, and John see only Jesus.

As the disciples come down from the mountaintop, Jesus tells them not to speak of this event until after he has risen from the dead. And although they do as Jesus asks, they also continue to discuss among themselves what he means by "to rise from the dead."

The sacrifice of God's Son on the cross frames the vision witnessed on the mountaintop. The cross may frighten us, as it confused and frightened Jesus' first followers. It should frighten us. The cross is also, however frightening, the core of our faith.

Questions for Reflection

• Who or what is most dear to you? How does God demand that you loosen your grasp on the person, persons, or things dearest to you?

• When God calls, how often do you say "I am ready"?

• What power anywhere in the world can possibly harm you? How well do your experiences and especially your fears agree with the second reading's insistence that nothing can harm you? What will you need to trust this insistence more than you already do?

• With what special insights or favors has God seemed to bless you? How does the cross frame them, and help you to understand them?

THIRD SUNDAY OF LENT, YEAR A READINGS

Thirsts

(These texts replace those of year B in parishes preparing elect for Easter baptisms; all parishes have the option of using these readings.)

[March 2, 1997; March 26, 2000; March 2, 2003]

The scrutinies are celebrated on the third, fourth, and fifth Sundays in Lent. The elect—persons in the final stages of preparation for baptism—stand before the community, who pray with and for them, in order that any remaining impediments to the gospel may be removed from their lives. In each scrutiny Christians and elect scrutinize all of their behavior over against the love of Jesus Christ. Inevitably, these rites confront people with hard questions. They are the primary means through which the community directs and supports the elect as they continue their long lenten retreat. They are also a powerful directive and support for the Christian faithful.

The first scrutiny is celebrated on the third Sunday of Lent. Its prayers and symbols embody our radical dependence upon the living water that Jesus offers. It is always to be prefaced by a proclamation of John 4.

First Reading: Exodus 17:3–7

I will be standing there in front of you....

After the excitement of their escape from pharaoh's army has worn off, the people grumble against Moses. Thirst drives them to nostalgia for the not-so-good old days in Egypt. They wonder what good their freedom can be, if they are merely going to die in the desert. Crying out to God, Moses is instructed to strike a rock with his staff. Water will flow for people to drink. Moses follows the instructions, in the presence of the elders of Israel, and the place receives a name commemorating the Israelites' quarreling and testing, concerning the Lord's presence in their midst.

Responsorial Psalm: Psalm 95:1–2, 6–7, 8–9

Second Reading: Romans 5:1–2, 5–8

Christ died for us.

The significance of the water featured in the other two readings is made explicit in these verses about the abundant, overflowing, life-giving grace that has been poured into our hearts through the Holy Spirit. Christ's death on our behalf is the foundation for our hope, our faith, the grace and love given to us, and the continued sustenance of the Spirit.

Gospel: John 4:5–42

...whoever drinks the water I give...will never be thirsty....

Traveling through Samaria, Jesus arrives one day at noon at the site of Jacob's well. A woman approaches, and Jesus asks her for water. What follows is a dialog in which the woman begins by toying with Jesus. Before long, however, she can see that he knows her better than she knows herself, and she drops all her defenses. She runs off to invite acquaintances to come and hear Jesus for themselves, and she returns with a crowd. Many hear for themselves, and they believe.

The dialog between Jesus and the woman uses the common experience of thirst to represent all the deepest yearnings of the human heart. The woman wants water, so she totes a bucket in the noonday sun. She wants love, so she has married five men and now consorts with a sixth. She wants religious truth, so she debates with Jesus about remembered stories common to Samaritan and Jew. Jesus accompanies her as she expresses her yearnings, and he promises to satisfy each one. He looks into her soul and tells her everything she ever did. She comes to know that he really can give living water.

The ironies in the story strip away all of our pretenses, too. It is the Samaritan, the despised sibling, who believes. As if to sharpen the point, a whole community of Samaritans comes into faith while the privileged disciples miss everything. A response to a simple request for a drink becomes a life-changing act of hospitality. Barriers drawn by gender, social standing, nationality, and religion are stripped away, so that only worship in Spirit and truth remain. With this text we proclaim Jesus standing before us insisting: "Give me a drink."

Questions for Reflection

•When were you really thirsty? What was it like? What satisfied your thirst?

•When did Jesus most recently ask you for a drink? How did he ask, and through whom? How did you respond?

•How would you relate to someone who knows all of your secrets?

•What is worship in Spirit and truth? In what ways does it differ from your usual ways of praying, of thinking, of behaving?

THIRD SUNDAY OF LENT

Obeying God

[March 2, 1997; March 26, 2000; March 2, 2003]
(In parishes where elect will be baptized at Easter, year A readings replace these)

First Reading: Exodus 20:1–17

I, the Lord, am your God....

Even Catholics who claim not to know the Bible recognize this text and its relative, Deuteronomy 5:6–21. In a pause after the narrow escape from Egypt, God gives Moses what we now call the decalogue, or "ten commandments." For more than three thousand years, these laws have been the foundation of morality and ethics for millions of people.

The text also reminds us of the bedrock upon which that foundation rests, because unless we are ever-careful, we can turn even rules given by God into idols. More than half of these verses are focused on God, detailing what we abbreviate into our first three commandments. God has subdued all natural and political forces to lead the people out of slavery. No form of idolatry should be permitted to divert our attention from this gigantic and powerful God who nonetheless always allows us our free choices. The people must honor God's name, never using it frivolously or, worse, for evil purposes. The sabbath must be kept holy: The people must imitate their unseen God, resting even as God has rested.

The remaining laws describe concrete social ways in which the people must honor and obey God. Parents are to be respected always, as are families, and especially the holy commitments that bind spouses to one another. The people must not kill or commit any dishonesty, or envy the possessions of others.

Responsorial Psalm: Psalm 19:8, 9, 10, 11

Second Reading: 1 Corinthians 1:22–25

...we preach Christ crucified....

The first letter to the church at Corinth is usually regarded as the most mature expression of Paul's thought. These short verses reflect both the essential dynamic in Christian faith and the early history of the movement that would become the church, during which many who hear of Christ fail to believe. The core of the gospel is a stumbling block to some, an absurdity to others: We preach Christ crucified. For Paul, this is the essence of Jewish tradition. Even so, some Jews trip and fall over the cross. Likewise, the cross makes no sense to Greeks, most likely persons engaged in the many varieties of philosophy and pagan belief. But some are called, and they see God's power and wisdom revealed in Christ.

Gospel: John 2:13–25
....in three days I will raise it up.

Jesus makes a whip and drives merchants and money changers from the temple precincts. As he overturns their tables, he yells "Stop turning my Father's house into a marketplace!" When challenged about his authority to do this, Jesus dares his challengers to "destroy this temple," which he will raise up in three days. They challenge him further, since the temple had taken forty-six years to build. No one on the scene understands, but later the disciples associate this event with his resurrection.

Although the episode is fascinating, the evangelist intends it mostly to set the stage for a larger drama. This is Jesus' first appearance in Jerusalem, at the Passover. Through John's account Jesus goes to Jerusalem for other festivals (chapters 5 and 7, and for the last time in chapter 12). In each visit, the temple plays an important role. With each successive visit, Jesus encounters greater resistance in the symbolic heart of Jewish tradition and religion. And John concludes the description of this first visit with an ominous awareness: Although many believed in Jesus' name, he would not trust himself to them because he knew what was in their hearts.

Like the first reading, this episode reminds us of what really matters. It insists that we honor and obey God, and it does so in terms of John's first prediction of the resurrection. As in the second reading, Jesus' resurrection is the most important actor's most important act, the perfect example of honor and obedience to God. And because it is only a harbinger of the great drama to come, this text invites us into a similar honor and obedience.

Questions for Reflection

• How do you keep yourself focused on God alone? What other gods clamor for your attention? How do you deal with them?

• How well do you honor your parents? Your children?

• How do you respect the lives and property of others?

• How honest are you, with regard to telling the truth, and especially in your commitment to your spouse?

• What sort of cross must you bear? How do you deal with it?

FOURTH SUNDAY OF LENT, YEAR A READINGS

Seeing

(These texts replace those of year B in parishes preparing elect for Easter baptisms; all parishes have the option of using these readings.)

[March 9, 1997; April 2, 2000; March 9, 2003]

First Reading: 1 Samuel 16:1b, 6–7, 10–13a

...the Lord looks into the heart.

These verses present an abridged version of the selection of David as the Lord's king of Israel. Saul, the first king, is paranoid and probably insane. He must be replaced, and the Lord has told Samuel to anoint one of the sons of Jesse. To elude Saul's suspicions, Samuel travels under the pretext of performing a sacrifice, taking a heifer to Bethlehem.

Reviewing each of the sons, Samuel guesses incorrectly. At last Jesse summons the youngest, and the Lord tells Samuel that this David will be king. God does not see as we see, because we look at appearances, while God looks into the heart.

Responsorial Psalm: Psalm 23:1–3, 3–4, 5, 6

Second Reading: Ephesians 5:8–14

...now you are light in the Lord.

The author introduces a simple and powerful image. The Christians at Ephesus once dwelt in darkness, but now they are children of light. Light produces every kind of goodness and justice and truth, while "vain deeds done in darkness" must produce evil, injustice, and falsehood.

The reading concludes by reciting a formula prayer that was probably well known to the original audience through baptism liturgies: "Awake, O sleeper, arise from the dead, and Christ will give you light."

Gospel: John 9:1–41

I am the light of the world.

A simple and yet astonishing act lies at the core of a drama exploring the struggle between light and darkness. Here Jesus, the light of the world, wins several victories over darkness. First, he accomplishes a healing unparalleled in ancient times. Second, he illustrates the overwhelming power of God's glory, vanquishing sin, which stands no chance. Third, the behavior of authorities shows them to remain, in every way, in the dark.

Encountering a man blind since birth, the disciples ask Jesus a question steeped in law: Is he blind because of his sin, or because of a sin of his ancestors? (See Exodus 20:5.) Jesus introduces a third possibility: The man is blind in order that God's works might be revealed in him. Then, spitting on the ground, Jesus makes mud, which he rubs on the man's eyes. When the man obeys Jesus' order to wash, he sees.

The man's troubles have just begun. Astonished neighbors demand an explanation, which he cannot give. He can only describe his experience. The neighbors take him to the authorities, who debate the theological significance of the miracle, question the man's parents to verify the circumstances of his birth, and interrogate the man a second time. Placing Jesus on trial by proxy, they demand to hear the man's story again. He states explicitly the drama's central point: You do not know who Jesus is, but only God can accomplish what he has done. And they evict him from the synagogue. In a final scene, the man sees Jesus for the first time. Professing his belief, he bows in worship.

It is an unfortunate fact of Christian existence that John's gospel casts Jesus' victory over the authorities in anti-Jewish terms. Today we must recognize this bias in John's text, and correct similar tendencies in ourselves. To perpetuate anti-Jewishness or any other form of racism is to dwell in precisely the darkness that Jesus has cast out.

This story connects light, life, and baptism. To refuse to believe is to remain in darkness, to continue in sin; but to believe is to see. The story also makes a subtle point. To be sure, God's works are revealed when the man washes his eyes in the pool. But they are revealed more clearly as he narrates his experience and grows into a profession of faith.

The second scrutiny invites us to allow Christ's light to illuminate every last nook and cranny in our lives. It celebrates the miracle of light in our lives, and the even greater miracle of the elect professing their faith before the world. It insists that we stop pretending to see when we do not, and open our eyes.

Questions for Reflection

•What are your "deeds done in darkness"? What are you called to do about them?

•How and where did your faith begin? How was your faith tested early, and how have you been tested more recently?

•How do you see God working in the lives of people around you, and in your own life?

FOURTH SUNDAY OF LENT

Believing

[March 9, 1997; April 2, 2000; March 9, 2003]

(In parishes where elect will be baptized at Easter, year A readings replace these)

First Reading: 2 Chronicles 36:14–17, 19–23

...and may his God be with him!

This reading interprets the final collapse of David's kingdom. It parallels descriptions given elsewhere in the Bible (see 2 Kings 24 and 25). Five and a half centuries before the birth of Christ, the kingdom of Judah fell to the Babylonians. Here the Chronicler insists that the collapse and subsequent captivity of the people henceforth known as "Jews" has been punishment for the repeated infidelity of prince, priest, and people, and for their abuse of God's prophets.

The Chronicler also interprets the actions of Cyrus, the Persian who overthrew Babylon and set the Jews free. He restored them to their homeland in gratitude to the God who gave him all the world. The pagan Cyrus is therefore seen as an agent of God's mercy.

Responsorial Psalm: Psalm 137:1–2, 3, 4–5, 6

Second Reading: Ephesians 2:4–10

This is not your doing, it is God's gift.

From the beginning the church has insisted that we do not save ourselves. These verses tell us that we ought not to take pride in anything we have or are or do, because what matters is God's gift to us. This message may be especially difficult to hear in the United States, home of the self-made man and the individualist. Yet we must hear it. God's mercy is given freely, not to reward anything we accomplish.

Gospel: John 3:14–21

God so loved the world that he gave his only Son....

How often have you seen "John 3:16" displayed at a televised sporting event? The verse is a favorite of those people who use loud and aggressive tactics to express what they call Christian faith. They try to persuade the rest of us that they know something that we do not know, and that our welfare depends upon our coming to see things their way.

There is nothing wrong with the message in the cited verse. On the contrary, it is very right: "God loved the world so much that God gave God's only Son, in order that anyone who believes in him may not die but instead may have eternal life." Problems arise, however, when a statement of truth is torn from its context and displayed glibly on national television. You could get the impression that if you want eternal life, you have only to say that you believe, as if believing were as easy as switching channels with your remote control.

It is not nearly so easy. As today's second reading insists, we are saved by God's favor alone, not by anything we do or say. But we cannot just do whatever feels good while waiting for God to zap us with what we consider unmistakable proof of our salvation. The fatal mistake in both lines of thinking is that in each case we remain always in control, beckoning God to do what we want. But such a remote-control "god" is not God at all. It is an especially sneaky and destructive idol, not the God of whom Jesus speaks in this text.

One Nicodemus, a Pharisee, has come to speak with Jesus in secret. Jesus insists that to see the kingdom of God, one must be born of water and Spirit. This phrase reflects what John and John's audience practiced: The church baptized persons who had been molded in Christ's image through service and prayer. Today's text begins in the middle of the conversation. As Moses lifted up an image of the serpent that was killing the Israelites in order to heal these who would gaze upon it (Numbers 21:8), the Son of Man must be lifted up to give eternal life to anyone who believes. The Son has not come to condemn, but to save. The light has come into darkness. Anyone who acts in truth comes into the light.

This cascade of images tells Nicodemus and us to respond to Jesus on many levels at once. We must trust him as if our lives depended on him, for they do. We must discover what it is to act in truth, and we must do it. We must love the light that illuminates everything we think, say, and do. We must allow ourselves to be born of water and Spirit, guided in a community. And we must state plainly what our actions tell the world, that we believe in him.

Questions for Reflection

•What persons, things, or events has God used to accomplish God's purposes in our world? With what persons, things, or events has God directed you?

•How well do you like a message that says that you cannot be a self-made person? How does this message affirm you, your thinking, and your choices? How does it challenge you? How will you respond to it?

•How would an impartial jury judge your belief? What evidence tells the world that you do believe? What evidence says something else?

FIFTH SUNDAY OF LENT
YEAR A READINGS

Spirit and life

(These texts replace those of year B in parishes preparing elect for Easter baptisms; all parishes have the option of using these readings.)

[March 16, 1997; April 9, 2000; March 16, 2003]

First Reading: Ezekiel 37:12–14

Then you shall know that I am the Lord.

Ezekiel is led by the hand of the Lord into a plain filled with bones. Instructed to call out to the bones, he follows instructions and witnesses some of the most astonishing events portrayed anywhere in the world's literature. Bone joins upon bone, sinews upon skeleton, flesh upon sinew, and skin upon flesh. Most importantly, God commands "spirit" to enter those who have been slain, and Ezekiel beholds an army. These visions are interpreted: The bones are the people of Israel, soon to return from exile.These verses issue God's climactic promise: "I will open your graves and command you to rise from them. I will place my spirit in you and settle you upon your land."

Responsorial Psalm: Psalm 130:1–2, 3–4, 5–6, 7–8

Second Reading: Romans 8:8–11

...the Spirit of God dwells in you.

With troublesome language Paul distinguishes between "flesh" and "spirit." Anyone "in the flesh" cannot please God. But Paul's audience is "in the spirit." If Christ is in you, the body is dead because of sin. We might think that these verses devalue our human bodies and our interactions with the world around us. But the last verse insists that the one who raised Christ from the dead will bring our mortal bodies to life also, through the Spirit dwelling within us. To be "in the spirit" is to value our bodies, our whole lives, and the whole lives of others.

How can we be in the spirit? The strongest clue is Paul's insistence that the spirit lives because of justice. But justice occurs in earthy, embodied situations: It cannot be abstract. We do justice when we feed the hungry and when we give shelter to the homeless person, to name just two examples. To name another, we do justice when we help the hungry and the homeless to provide for themselves. To be in the spirit is to work always for justice, animated by God's own Spirit. It is to keep the promises we made, or which were made on our behalf, or which we will make very soon at Easter, at our baptisms.

Gospel: John 11:1–45

I am the resurrection and the life....

Lazarus has died, and his friend Jesus is led to the burial place. Troubled in spirit and moved by the deepest emotions, Jesus directs the stone to be moved from the tomb. He offers a prayer of thanksgiving (*eucharisto*) to the Father, and calls Lazarus out. As the first reading illustrates, only God can do such a thing. When the dead man appears, Jesus tells the crowd to remove the burial cloths from him. And many people place their faith in Jesus.

This narrative climaxes the cycle of stories that accompany the scrutinies. Truths represented metaphorically in the stories of the Samaritan woman and the man born blind are made explicit in this one. Jesus who gives living water and light also brings the dead to life. Jesus fills our deepest yearnings and illumines the darkest recesses of our souls. Most importantly, he brings life to the most hopeless and seemingly irreversible of situations.

This is the core of our faith. Doctrines and creeds express realities that transform the lives of those who profess those words. But doctrines and creeds are not themselves these transforming realities. Sometimes we resist Christ's genuine and constant offer of life. We live in the flesh, not in the spirit.

The story also illustrates the role of the community in the faith of the individual person. God alone gives life and faith and satisfies our deepest thirsts. Still, the community must unbind the person who has been set free. In this important respect, the story of Lazarus contrasts with that of the man born blind. In the latter story, the man comes into faith despite being abandoned by neighbors, parents, and authorities. Here we see a community responding properly to Jesus' gift of life, and we are challenged to act in a similar manner.

Questions for Reflection

•What dead ends do you encounter? What situations do you find most hopeless? How often do you ask God to bring life to these situations?

•In what ways do you sometimes impose limits upon God's work? How does your parish inhibit God's work? How do your neighborhood, your town, your society frustrate God's intentions? What can you do about these limitations? What will you do about them?

•When and how do you give thanks to God?

FIFTH SUNDAY OF LENT

Now!

[March 16, 1997; April 9, 2000; March 16, 2003]
(In parishes where elect will be baptized at Easter, year A readings replace these)

First Reading: Jeremiah 31:31–34

I will be their God and they shall be my people.

At the end of his prophetic career Jeremiah sees the futility of his many warnings to the chosen people. He has witnessed some of the most turbulent chapters in history, as kings and empires have come and gone. And despite his best efforts he has seen the fall of Jerusalem, the end of the kingdom of Judah, and the beginning of his people's captivity.

Living his last days in Egypt, Jeremiah is not willing to give up. He composes these words: "The day will come when I will make a new covenant with my people, says the Lord. Unlike the old covenant it will be unbreakable. I will place my law within them and write it on their hearts. They will not have to teach, because everyone shall know me. And I will forgive them and remember their sin no more."

Responsorial Psalm: Psalm 51:3–4, 12–13, 14–15

Second Reading: Hebrews 5:7–9

...he learned obedience from what he suffered.

Probably referring to Gethsemane, the author describes Jesus in the flesh, offering prayers with cries and tears. Christ has known suffering and has learned obedience through it. Now, perfected, he offers salvation to all who obey him.

Gospel: John 12:20–33

Now is the time....

While all four gospels describe aspects of Jesus' ministry and passion, John's narrates the least action and presents the greatest amount of talk. In the other accounts, especially in Mark, events often speak for themselves. In this book, events always provoke talk about their significance.

Having raised Lazarus (John 11), and having left Bethany after an anointing that Judas pronounces wasteful (12:1–7), Jesus has come to Jerusalem. His entry is a crisis for Jewish leaders, who see what seems to be the whole world going after him (12:9–11, 19).

Now people identified only as "some Greeks" want to see him. They may be Gentiles, representing the world coming to Jesus, and amplifying what John wants us to see as a Jewish crisis. Jesus talks: "The time has come for my glorification. If a grain of wheat falls to the earth and dies, it produces [see 1 Corinthians 15:36]. If you hold onto your life, you will lose it, while if you let go of your life you preserve it eternally [also Mark 8:35, Matthew 10:39 and 16:25, and Luke 9:24; 17:33]. To serve me, you must follow me. I am troubled by the prospect of what I must do, yet it is my purpose." A voice from heaven interrupts Jesus' soliloquy, and people hear it in various ways, some as thunder, others as an angel speaking only to Jesus. He resumes and concludes: "Now is the time of judgment. When I am lifted up, I will draw everyone to myself."

In this talk Jesus announces that now is the appointed time. He does this three times (23, 27, 31), perhaps following the patterns of Hebrew poetry, but in any case emphasizing his point. All of his signs and teachings have led to this "hour." And what is this hour? John spells it out in the remainder of his account, which is fully half the book. Jesus' opponents engineer his arrest and execution, but he rises from the dead and appears to the apostles. But, as always, John is concerned with the many directions from which we might approach this truth. He portrays Jesus talking about the significance of this event. We might see Jesus glorified. We might gain insight into his cross as a dying and fruitful grain of wheat. We might hear his invitation to lose our lives in order to gain them. We might appreciate the depths to which he is troubled by the cross.

Most of all, we might hear the urgency of this hour: Now is the time for us to decide to follow Jesus. However much the cross may disturb us, whatever we see or fail to see, Jesus calls us now to let go of our lives. Now is the hour.

Questions for Reflection

•What are your dead ends? What situations, events, and relationships seem hopeless? How does God handle our dead ends? What does Jeremiah tell us?

•How does Jesus offer life to you? How do you receive it? What concrete things do you do? How do you resist Jesus' gift of life?

•There are no excuses: Now is the hour. How does this hour trouble you? What is your cross? How do you see Jesus glorified? How do you let go of your life?

PASSION SUNDAY (PALM SUNDAY)

The Cross

[March 23, 1997; April 16, 2000; March 23, 2003]

Procession: Mark 11:1–10

Blessed be he who comes in the name of the Lord!

We proclaim and reenact Jesus' entry into Jerusalem in order to immerse ourselves in the drama of his passion. With the disciples we find a colt for Jesus to ride, evoking Zechariah's description of the coming king (9:9). With the crowds, we spread branches on Jesus' path. With our ancestors, we sing Hosanna! God save us! With Christians throughout history and over the whole world we enter the great drama anew.

First Reading: Isaiah 50:4–7

The Lord God is my hope.

The church has always viewed Jesus as the "suffering servant" described in the book of Isaiah. That book's third servant song sets the tone for today's long gospel proclamation. The servant has used God-given gifts in a faithful manner, teaching, healing, and assisting others. And when asked to suffer, the servant has submitted.

The closing verse offers a hint of the glory of the cross: The Lord God is my help, therefore I am not disgraced; I have set my face like flint, knowing that I shall not be put to shame.

Responsorial Psalm: Psalm 22:8–9, 17–18, 19–20, 23–24

The first line of this psalm serves as the choral response. Its words are Jesus' last, in the passion according to Mark: "My God, why have you forsaken me?"

Second Reading: Philippians 2:6–11

God highly exalted him.

These verses constitute an early Christian hymn. Probably sung at liturgies, the hymn proclaims our most basic beliefs. Christ is God's equal, but he emptied himself, having been born in our likeness. As one of us, he accepted everything that came his way, even death on the cross. And because of this obedient death, God has glorified Jesus and directed all creation to worship him.

Paul has added to the hymn, insisting that our attitude must be Christ's. We must empty ourselves, allow ourselves to be humbled, and accept even suffering as we serve our God and the well-being of all creatures.

Gospel: Mark 14:1–15:47
My God, my God, why have you abandoned me?

Today we proclaim the oldest and most important part of our oldest account of the gospel. Like countless generations before us, we tell Jesus' story, which is also our story. The account of the last supper and the arrest, trial, and death of our Lord is not merely a history. It also defines us and our way of life. We read the passion as drama to accentuate the truths we celebrate at every Eucharist: We are the ones whom Jesus nourishes, who follow his example, who are called to the cross.

While Mark's account of the gospel is considerably shorter than the others, his passion story is as long as those of the other evangelists. Each author embellishes the basic story in a distinct way. In general, Mark's account is the most stark and matter-of-fact. It also seems to portray the disciples most harshly. A subtle detail illustrates their complete abandonment of Jesus: At the moment of death, he speaks Aramaic, his native language and that of his closest associates. Yet as Mark tells us, no one who hears can understand what he says (15:34–36). He has been abandoned utterly, executed among strangers who are just doing their jobs.

As Jesus dies, the beginning of Psalm 22 is on his lips. The psalm begins in tones of despair, but it concludes in an unshakable confidence that God redeems. In his dying words, Jesus invites us into that same confidence.

Questions

• Why do we recite this drama every year? Why should you enter into and participate in the drama of the passion? Why shouldn't you remain a spectator?

• How does your attitude resemble Christ's? How does your attitude differ from Christ's? How must you change? How will you change?

• What role best fits you, in the drama that is Christ's passion? If your neighborhood theater were staging the passion and casting people according to the real-life personalities, would you be Jesus, or Pilate, or Peter, or Judas, or someone else? Why does the role you choose fit you better than others?

• How does the drama of the passion take shape in your life? What cross do you carry? How do you carry it? What help do you enlist? What additional help do you need?

Chrism Mass

Renewal

[Ordinarily on Holy Thursday, the Chrism Mass is scheduled by the bishop between Passion Sunday and the Mass of the Lord's Supper.]

The priests and people of every diocese worship with their bishop on this occasion each year. The priests renew their commitment to ordained ministry and concelebrate the Eucharist. All witness the consecration of the holy oils. The Chrism Mass is a feast of symbols, a final preparation for the climax, which is the Easter Triduum.

The symbols embodied at this Mass follow ancient practice: The oil to be used for sacramental anointing of the sick is blessed first. The oil of catechumens follows. It is to be used for exorcisms and to strengthen catechumens in public rites as they journey toward Easter. Lastly, the bishop consecrates Chrism. Having mixed balsam or other perfume into the oil, he breathes upon the mixture and recites a prayer evoking the place of oil at crucial points in Hebrew and Christian history. This prayer also reminds us of connections between oil and water. Chrism is to be used to anoint neophytes at their baptisms, and for all other confirmations. It is also used to anoint the hands of priests when they are ordained.

However powerful, these rites are purposely incomplete. They set the stage for our Easter celebration. Because priests are servants, the renewal of their priesthood can only be fulfilled out among the faithful. Because we are all God's servants, our annual renewal thrusts us into a world hungry for the gospel.

First Reading: Isaiah 61:1–3, 6, 8–9
You yourselves shall be named priests of the Lord.

The one who has been anointed speaks these words recorded in the third, pseudonymously written portion of the book of Isaiah. The first verse describes connections among God's spirit and a person, and God's anointing. This anointing has a purpose: bring glad tidings; heal; proclaim liberty...and release; announce a year of favor; comfort; give a glorious mantle. The anointed, not identified by the author, and probably the entire community of Israel recently returned from exile, is what we might call today an "enabler" or a "facilitator." The whole congregation, modern as well as ancient, hears the divine intent: "You are priests...ministers, exemplars before your children and the nations of the world." We may find in these words a job description for our priests, but also for the whole church.

Responsorial Psalm: Psalm 89:21–22, 25, 27

Second Reading: Revelation 1:5–8
I am the Alpha and the Omega.
The fiery, visionary tone of much of the book of Revelation is absent in these verses, which sound more like Paul. They come from the book's introduction, and, like the first reading, they define the audience as a "priestly people." Here the agent of God's anointing is Jesus Christ, the firstborn from the dead and the ruler of all kings. Jesus anoints especially through his sacrifice. An apocalyptic tone emerges in verse 7, which echoes Daniel 7:13 and Zechariah 12:10: "Look, he is coming among the clouds, and everyone will see him, even those who killed him."

Gospel: Luke 4:16–21
The spirit of the Lord is upon me....
Jesus has faced down the devil in the long desert retreat following his baptism. Now he begins his public life. We catch a glimpse of him in his home synagogue, at Capernaum, where his emerging reputation has preceded him (4:14–15). He reads exactly those verses that comprise today's first reading, and they are familiar to the congregation. He begins a sermon with the matter-of-fact statement: Today this passage is fulfilled in your presence. For his trouble, he is expelled from the synagogue (4:28–30).

Jesus' example is audacious, even offensive to some. It is exactly this audacity which seals his fate later, when he faces the Sanhedrin in Jerusalem (22:71). The Easter Triduum celebrates Jesus' unwavering faithfulness to the anointed's ancient purpose. His priestly people are called to a similar audacity, invited into the same purpose.

Questions for Reflection
• Who is overlooked in our world? Think hard. Who needs to hear glad tidings? Who needs to be healed? Who is held captive?

• How can you improve the ways in which you announce the good news, heal, and set captives free? What specific steps will you take, right away?

• How do these readings help you to define your vocation? What will you do during this Holy Week to renew your vocation?

EASTER TRIDUUM
HOLY THURSDAY,
MASS OF THE LORD'S SUPPER
Servanthood

[March 27, 1997; April 20, 2000; March 27, 2003]

First Reading: Exodus 12:1–8, 11–14
This day shall be a memorial feast for you....

This text describe the conditions in which Jews must celebrate the Seder at Passover. While the Bible contains other, more detailed descriptions of the ritual (Leviticus 23:5–8; Numbers 9:2–5; Numbers 28:16ff.; Deuteronomy 16:1–8), this one achieves special impact by virtue of its location in the biblical narrative. As of Exodus 12, the Israelites are still in bondage. Nine plagues have been visited upon Egypt, and God has informed Moses of the tenth plague.

The Seder did not assume final shape until, at the earliest, the Jews' return to Palestine from Babylonian captivity, *circa* 520 BCE. We read this description where an editor has placed it, so that we might see it as a vital part of God's revelation to Moses. The ritual is to be seen as God's expectation, an integral part of the fight for freedom.

All diners must be dressed for flight. The blood of the lamb must mark Hebrew homes, for God will execute judgment on Egypt's inferior "gods" by striking all of Egypt's firstborn children.

Most people today do not like the idea of a bloodthirsty God slaying children to bend Egypt to the divine will. We should understand that the narrative describes a holy war conducted more than a millennium before Jesus' time, and that violence is a divine last resort. Here, God is warrior. Israel participates in the holy war not by committing violence, but by celebrating the Seder.

Responsorial Psalm: Psalm 116:12–13, 15–16, 17–18

Second Reading: 1 Corinthians 11:23–26
Do this in remembrance of me.

These are the "words of institution" of the Eucharist. Paul has situated them in the middle of a section correcting Corinthian abuses that have been brought to his attention. The entire eleventh chapter of the book deals with proper conduct at worship, with a focus on the divisions and attitudes that have corrupted Corinthian liturgies. The apostle condemns these divisions (11:17–22).

Here he describes the authentic tradition (literally, "that which is handed over") in which the Lord's Supper is celebrated. Citing Jesus' own words according to what has been handed over to him, Paul urges the church to eat the bread and drink the cup. These are Christ's body and blood, consumed in remembrance of him, and that is why we worship. It is pointless, and in fact sinful, to gather without this single purpose, as the rest of the chapter illustrates. This is the foundation of the eucharistic theology upon which the four evangelists have built their accounts of the gospel.

Gospel: John 13:1–15
...as I have done, so you must do.

Jesus and disciples sit at table *before* the feast of the Passover. Where other evangelists describe Jesus breaking bread (Matthew 26:26–29; Mark 14:22–25; Luke 22:15–20), John portrays him washing the feet of the disciples. Over Peter's objections, Jesus describes the work of the church: "If I washed your feet, I who am 'teacher' and 'Lord,' then you must do the same."

For John, who compresses various themes, the meal is synonymous with servanthood. This narrative of Jesus as servant at the last supper is an essential portion of John's understanding of Eucharist. We reenact Jesus' foot-washing at this Mass of the Lord's Supper to complete the formal renewal of priestly vows inaugurated at the Chrism Mass. We remove the consecrated species from the tabernacle and strip the altar of its garments to draw attention to the Eucharist. After John's example, we accentuate the meal by its removal. To participate in the Lord's supper, we must not only cast aside our divisions and focus our entire selves upon Christ's body and blood. In common with our ordained leaders, we must also recommit ourselves to serve. To eat is to become servants.

Questions for Reflection

•How do you like the image of God as warrior? What images would you prefer? How will you make room in your heart for all of the Bible's various descriptions of God?

•How do you approach the eucharistic table? What must you change? What kind of support do you need, to make any necessary changes?

•How has Jesus been your servant? How do you serve others? How can you act more faithfully as servant?

EASTER TRIDUUM
GOOD FRIDAY,
CELEBRATION OF THE LORD'S PASSION
Dying
[March 28, 1997; April 21, 2000; March 28, 2003]

Church law prohibits Mass on this day. There are three parts in this service: a liturgy of the word, which includes litanies of intercessory prayers; veneration of the cross; and communion, using species consecrated at Holy Thursday's Mass of the Lord's Supper.

First Reading: Isaiah 52:13–53:12
Yet it was our infirmities that he bore, our sufferings that he endured.
Here is the entire fourth song of God's servant, the work of "Second Isaiah." From the beginning, the church has recognized Jesus in these phrases: "...So marred was his look ... He was spurned and avoided ... A man of suffering, accustomed to infirmity ... We held him in no esteem ... Yet it was our sins he bore, our sufferings he endured ... He was pierced for our offenses, crushed for our sins ... Like a lamb to the slaughter ... A grave was assigned to him among the wicked ... Though he had done no wrong ... The will of the Lord shall be accomplished through him ... He shall take away the sins of many and win pardon for their offenses." In magnificent poetry the prophet sets forth what becomes later the core of the Christian creed.

We ought not to suppose that, five centuries early, the author intended these words to speak of Jesus of Nazareth. Still, it is appropriate that we use them on this day, for the author probably envisioned a future servant, a messiah ("anointed," literally "oily one") in whose suffering all would be redeemed.

Responsorial Psalm: Psalm 31:2, 6, 12–13, 15–16, 17, 25

Second Reading: Hebrews 4:14–16; 5:7–9
...he learned obedience from what he suffered....
These verses identify Jesus Christ as the servant described in the first reading. Christian doctrine is also stated explicitly: Tempted in every

way, he never sinned; When perfected, he offered salvation to all who obey him; He learned obedience through suffering. Although no one wants to suffer, this text shows us the way to salvation. We too learn obedience in suffering. Contrast this portrait with Holy Thursday's Exodus picture of God as warrior!

Gospel: John 18:1–19:42
I am he.

We can see much evidence in this text indicating that John was a literary and theological genius.

The passion begins and ends in a garden. The author echoes the Bible's account of human origins and purpose (Genesis 2:8) with this narrative device. In a similar manner, when apprehended by the crowd, Jesus asks "Whom do you seek?" echoing his own first words in this account of the gospel (1:38: "What do you seek?") His arrest closes that chapter of his ministry in which he walks freely and summons followers. A new chapter begins, one of extreme suffering and death.

Identifying himself, Jesus repeats the divine name, which is supposed to be uttered only once each year by a designated leader at Yom Kippur: "I am." (See John 18:5; 18:8; see also Exodus 3:14.) John identifies him explicitly with the Father, and in so doing recognizes the wedge that has already long since driven Jews and Christians apart.

The actions of the "other disciple" may be included as a foil for, and a contrast to, those of Peter. He follows Jesus to the bitter end, while Peter abandons the Lord, even to the extent of reversing God's name: "I am not!" (18:17; 18:25). Scholars argue that despite 21:24 this other disciple cannot have been the author. Any eyewitnesses were dead long before this gospel was composed.

Hauled in front of the authorities, Jesus turns the tables. He places everyone on trial. In Jesus' tribunal, Pilate appears a sympathetic figure. He is exonerated, and with him Rome is held blameless. It is not his fault that he cannot recognize the one who is the Truth standing before him. By contrast, "the Jews" are seen to manipulate their own law to accomplish Jesus' demise before the festival of the Passover. Their hypocrisy lies exposed before the innocent Jesus. They have engineered Jesus' death and tied Pilate's hands. The only decision he can make is to express his contempt for this people he must govern by labeling the crucified Jesus "King of the Jews."

Catholic doctrine condemns explicitly any form of anti-Jewish invective (*Nostra Aetate*, 4; *Catechism of the Catholic Church*, 839). We must read John's piercing ironies with this teaching in mind, and remember that the evangelist's purpose is not to blame, but to encourage faith. We must remember another irony: Peter, the first bishop of Rome, has played a role in Jesus' demise. This narrative asks us to recognize the One who is the Truth, and places us all in judgment before him.

Questions for Reflection

•How do you suffer? What do you do to avoid suffering? Who suffers, so that you do not have to suffer?

•If God is both suffering servant and warrior, where in between these two poles is your image of God? Do you see God more as servant or as warrior? What difference does your image of God make to your thoughts and actions?

•Although Jesus has not come to judge, his very presence causes us to evaluate ourselves. How well do you meet your responsibilities? What must you change?

EASTER TRIDUUM
VIGIL
Go now and tell

[March 29, 1997; April 22, 2000; March 29, 2003]

The Easter Vigil as we know it was inaugurated by Pius XII in 1950. Its symbols and movements echo and condense the devotions our ancestors celebrated as they vigiled through the three days and nights of their Easter celebrations. Ancient practice culminated in baptisms at dawn. Our restored catechumenate has reclaimed this dimension, as well.

The Vigil begins in darkness, the congregation assembled outside the sanctuary. A bonfire chases away the dark and the cold, and the Easter candle is blessed and lit. The congregation processes to the baptismal pool, where the readings proclaim many of our best stories.

First Reading: Genesis 1:1–2:2
In the beginning....

The first of two creation stories narrates events of an unimaginably huge scale. The story sets forth a Hebrew cosmology, a "theory of everything."

In contrast to the cosmologies of other ancient peoples, here there are no divine battles: In the beginning...God created the heavens and the earth, with word, not by conquering another divinity. In five days, God commands into being light, arrangements of water and vegetation, the lights of the night sky, and creatures upon the earth. There are no skirmishes, only God's will and God's daily judgment that it is good. On the sixth day God creates the human person in the divine image, male and female. Now, before the sabbath rest, God says it is *very* good. Human beings are the climax of creation and, unique among creatures, God's image.

Responsorial Psalm: Psalm 104:1–2, 5–6, 10, 12, 13–14 24, 35 or Psalm 33:4–5, 6–7, 12–13, 20–22

Second Reading: Genesis 22:1–18

I will bless you abundantly....

This is the full text of the climactic story in the Abraham cycle, proclaimed in abridged form on the second Sunday of Lent, year B. Over against God's promises of countless descendants, Abraham learns that he must sacrifice his son, Isaac. It is an absurd and terrifying divine demand that seems to frustrate not only God's covenant with Abraham, but also the very purpose of creation.

This troublesome story narrates discernment and God's faithfulness. It is finally a contest between right faith and wrong faith. Most other gods demand human sacrifice (see 1 Kings 16:34, for example): Could Abraham imagine that his mysterious and magnificent God would do any less? Abraham bundles the child off to Moriah, responding faithfully to God's request. As his fatal blade begins its descent toward the child's neck, Abraham hears God's messenger: "Do not harm the boy." Having let go of his most cherished hopes, Abraham learns God's will: God cherishes us.

Responsorial Psalm: Psalm 16:5, 8, 9–10, 11

Third Reading: Exodus 14:15–15:1

...the Israelites marched into the midst of the sea on dry land.

The story of Israel's passage through the sea is practically guaranteed to bring an audience to its feet, cheering. It describes the formative event in Hebrew history. From beginning to end, God is in control. God makes pharaoh's heart obstinate, but at God's command Moses holds his hand over the sea, which parts for the chosen people. After Israel has passed through the sea safely, God directs Moses to stretch out his hands again, and the Egyptian army is destroyed.

The exodus is a passage from slavery into freedom, but also a passage from a stratified order into wilderness, from begrudging dependence into independence and hardship. A community liberated by God must rely upon God for everything. Christ's passage from death to life echoes this saving event.

Responsorial Psalm: Exodus 15:1–2, 3–4, 5–6, 17–18

Fourth Reading: Isaiah 54:5–14

The Lord calls you back.

With this text's most important image, God describes the relationship between God and the people: "Your creator is your husband; you are like a wife abandoned in the husband's moment of anger." The image is not attractive at face value, but consider that, unlike any human husband, the creator-spouse is unfailingly righteous. God has allowed the people to be taken in exile because they have been a wayward and unfaithful spouse. God has never stopped loving this people and promises now never to rebuke them again.

This text comforts: "With great tenderness I will take you back.... My love shall never leave you.... Great shall be the peace of your children." God will not abandon the people, even if the natural order collapses. The climax is both promise and challenge: "You shall be established in justice." The people's past failures to do justice constituted the waywardness that an angry God punished with exile. Justice requires that they be restored to their home, but also that they become an ethical beacon for the rest of the world.

Responsorial Psalm: Psalm 30:2, 4, 5–6, 11–12, 13

Fifth Reading: Isaiah 55:1–11
All you who are thirsty, come to the water!
This is the climax of "Second Isaiah," but it does not include the chapter's final verses. God invites the audience to a meal at an oasis in the desert. "Do not waste your money on what cannot satisfy. Listen to God's word, and you will eat well." The meal renews the everlasting covenant. Even so, God's people cannot only look inward, for they are to be a sign of God's saving presence in the world.

The poet speaks of repentance both personal and corporate. If the scoundrel forsakes his ways, he accepts responsibility for the poor and the marginated. God forgives generously. The gulf between God's ways and our ways is enormous, like the distance between the heavens and the earth.

God's word is like water that journeys through the world with a purpose, and that returns to the heavens only after it has met its purpose. God's word is alive, pervasive, both life-giving and destructive, not confined to human words, available and vital at all times. The omitted verses complete this picture of God's banquet as a commissioning. "You will leave here in joy. You will return in peace, and all creation will sing and dance for you. You will be a sign, this meal will be a sign. God's joy and peace will govern the earth, because of you." Perhaps the Vigil's sacraments are meant to embody and enact these images.

Responsorial Psalm: Isaiah 12:2–3, 4, 5–6

Sixth Reading: Baruch 3:9–15, 32–4:4

Such is our God: No other is to be compared to God.

This text begins with the *Shema Israel*, the classic call to prayer, and it offers instruction to a people in exile. "You deserve your predicament," says the prophet, "because you have disobeyed God's wisdom." Some of the previous readings are summarized in hopes that Israel will learn the commandments of life, but the text is not an iteration of Mosaic law. It is instead a transition from the law into something new, a reliance not upon laws written in books, but upon wisdom.

Wisdom is personified, feminine in gender. She is the book of the precepts of God, a law that endures forever.

Responsorial Psalm: Psalm 19:8, 9, 10, 11

Seventh Reading: Ezekiel 36:16–28

I will give you a new heart and place a new spirit withing you.

Ugly imagery is used to describe the chosen people's tenure in the promised land: Their conduct was like the defilement of a menstruous woman. God acts, not for Israel's sake, but for God's own name, which Israel has profaned. God will restore this people and cleanse them in a ritual bath. God will replace their hearts of stone with natural hearts. God's spirit will dwell within them, and the evidence will be observed in their fidelity to divine statute. The promise is ancient and ever-new: You will be my people and I will be your God.

Responsorial Psalm: Psalm 42:3, 5; 43:3, 4
or Psalm 51:12–13: 14–15, 18–19

Epistle: Romans 6:3–11

…we too might live a new life.

These verses give Paul's interpretation of baptism, which is the framework for any understanding of Christian baptism. It is a burial with Christ, a burial that leads to new life. From now on, he tells his listeners, you are dead to sin, and alive through Jesus Christ.

Responsorial Psalm: Psalm 118:1–2, 16, 17, 22–23

Gospel: Mark 16:1–8

He has been raised up.

Our oldest gospel account portrays Mary Magdalene, Mary the mother of James, and Salome coming to the tomb to anoint Jesus' body. When they arrive, the stone has been rolled away. They enter. A herald greets them and instructs them: "Jesus is not here. He has been raised up. Go and tell the disciples that they will see him in Galilee." But overcome with fear, the women do not tell anyone.

This ending does not satisfy. If the women tell no one, then how can we have heard of the resurrection? Mark's account continues for eleven verses that the Roman Catholic church accepts as authentic and inspired. Even so, nearly everyone thinks of them as an addition to the oldest existing manuscripts, a harmonization of material contained in the newer accounts of Matthew and Luke. Some scholars suppose that Mark did write a more satisfactory ending, but it has never been found.

A truncated ending would be consistent with Mark's style. The shortest of our gospel accounts, Mark relies most heavily upon action, tending to de-emphasize preaching and teaching. Actions count far more than words. The action in this text is powerful enough. The women intend to anoint a corpse, but they find the tomb empty except for the herald. His words only astonish and scare them. We do not even learn whether they believe.

Maybe the ending *should* be no ending at all. Through the entire account, Mark has described events and evidence, expecting us to respond. This proclamation does not so much teach us as challenge. Here are the facts, it says. How do you respond? What ending do you write?

After the homily, we celebrate the responses of the elect, whose journeys culminate in the sacraments of initiation. The congregation prays over them, asking them publicly to renounce Satan, to profess their faith, and to declare whether they come to the sacrament freely. One by one, they are baptized, clothed in white garments, and confirmed. Now "neophytes," they lead the congregation into the sanctuary, where they witness and participate in the Eucharist for the first time. By their actions and words they tell all disciples, and all the world, that Christ is risen.

Questions for Reflection

•When has God's action silenced you? Why were you made silent? Were you inhibited by fear, or anger, or confusion, or something else? How have you managed to deal with God's action?

•What ending would you write for Mark's gospel? What story is told in your thoughts, words, and actions?

•What are the church's most important responsibilities? How do you help the church to do what together we must do?

•What makes someone a credible witness to the good news? How do you announce the good news? How can you do this more effectively, more credibly?

EASTER TRIDUUM
EASTER SUNDAY

The Story

[March 30, 1997; April 23, 2000; March 30, 2003]

First Reading: Acts 10:34, 37–43

I take it you know what has been reported....

In important ways, Peter's audience is just like us: We have heard of Jesus' resurrection. For us, as for them, there is a huge difference between hearing the story and becoming part of it. Summoned to the house of the centurion Cornelius, Peter acknowledges what those present have already heard, but he also sketches the Christian gospel: Beginning with the baptism John preached, Jesus did good works and healed all who were in the grip of the devil. Several witnesses can describe the wonders he performed. The authorities killed him, but God raised him up on the third day, as several witnesses can also attest. He ate with them and commissioned them to bear witness to him as the one set apart by God as judge of all.

Something is new. At the end of Peter's talk, in verses not included here, the whole crowd receives the Holy Spirit. We are not told how it happens, but we do see the effect. All believe in Jesus, and all are baptized. Their lives changed, they are now part of the gospel. We have heard this story countless times. Perhaps we are already part of the story, perhaps we remain spectators. Maybe this time there is something new?

Responsorial Psalm: Psalm 118:1–2, 16–17, 22–23

Second Reading: Colossians 3:1–4

...you have been raised up in company with Christ.

Once we have been raised up with Christ, we see the world in terms defined by the cross. We focus our attention on what the author calls "things above," because now our life is hidden, with Christ.

Alternate Second Reading: 1 Corinthians 5:6–8

Christ our Passover has been sacrificed.

Paul borrows imagery from the Seder, the Passover meal, to direct the actions and choices of Christians. Since even a bit of leaven affects the entire dough, get rid of it. The old leaven is corruption and wickedness. Let us be new bread of sincerity and truth.

Gospel: John 20:1–9
He saw and believed.

Before dawn Mary Magdalene sees that the stone has been rolled from the tomb. She summons Simon Peter, who runs with another disciple. This other arrives first, without entering. Simon Peter does enter and sees burial garments set aside, folded carefully. Then the other disciple enters, sees, and believes.

John's first resurrection story describes different ways in which we may express our belief. These ways may also be artful descriptions of stages in our growth in faith. Mary does not yet understand, but still on the basis of what she can see she announces the good news. Peter walks right in, and is enveloped in the greatest of all mysteries. The unnamed disciple pauses, observes, follows the example of another, and believes.

The truth is unwrapped slowly, just as it is in our lives. Sometimes we see compelling evidence, but all we can do is to run to find the help of others. At other times, we contemplate what stands before us. At still other times we must explore matters in great depth, without ever receiving the gift of belief. And at other times we simply see and believe.

The ways of belief narrated here suggest a vital role for the church, in Cornelius' first-century home and for us today. A glance at the empty tomb may move us, but alone it rarely yields either understanding or faith. Entering the tomb is important but difficult. Even Peter does not enter alone, but in the company of another. And the unnamed disciple believes after the church invites him into the empty tomb.

Questions for Reflection

• When did you first hear the good news of Christ risen? How many times have you heard this story? When did the story become your story, or if you have not yet entered it, what is keeping you a spectator? In the words of the second epistle reading, what is the leaven that you must replace? How do you intend to do this?

• Which of the three characters in this text best portrays your response to the central story of our lives? Do you run to announce the evidence, like Mary Magdalene? Do you walk right in, like Peter? Do you observe carefully before committing, like the unnamed disciple? What other responses are possible? How do you respond?

• How has the church helped your growth in faith? How will you assist others?

SECOND SUNDAY OF EASTER

Spirit, peace, authority, mission

[April 6, 1997; April 30, 2000; April 6, 2003]

First Reading: Acts 4:32–35

The community...were of one heart and one mind.

Here is an idealized portrait of the first generation of Christians. Possessed of one heart and one mind, the believers have forsaken private possessions and hold everything in common. They respect the apostles, who witness to the Lord's resurrection. No one is needy, because all who once owned property have sold it and given the proceeds to the apostles for distribution.

We cannot romanticize this picture of community, even if we find it attractive. Later chapters of the Acts of the Apostles illustrate complexities that make the picture impossible to maintain. Millennia later, we know even more complexities. Moreover, this is only a partial picture that represents the teaching and the community life of the primitive church. It overlooks the church's mission and worship. We cannot hope only to nourish ourselves, for the church is supposed to be much more than a collection of people who preserve teachings and who feel good together.

Still, the picture is valuable. Christ's victory is our victory. Easter is accomplished, new life has entered the world, and for a short time the baptized may rest in the great mysteries that envelop us. Before we follow the apostles to our next public act of responsibility, we may nurture and teach one another.

Responsorial Psalm: Psalm 118:2–4, 13–15, 22–24

Second Reading: 1 John 5:1–6

...the Spirit is truth.

Everyone who believes has been begotten by God. To love the father is to love the child. We love God's children when we do what we are commanded. This is the same as loving God. We who are begotten of God conquer the world. The conqueror is the one who believes in Jesus. Jesus Christ has come in water and blood. The Spirit testifies to this, and the Spirit is truth.

The logic of these verses is the same as that of most of Jesus' speeches, as John's gospel account portrays them. They seem to leap from one topic to the next, defying theme or main point. But the leaps are vital to John's logic. Our profession of faith is more than a pronouncement of words. We express many things at once: our status as God's children; our fidelity to the commandments; our conquest of the world.

Gospel: John 20:19–31
My Lord and my God!

This may be the most important text in the Bible. We read it on both the second Sunday of Easter and Pentecost in every year. It frames our Easter season. In it John recounts the risen Jesus' appearance to the disciples as they cower in fear behind locked doors.

Jesus offers one gift to the disciples, the Holy Spirit, the most valuable of all gifts. In the same logic seen in today's epistle reading, Jesus describes three aspects of the gift. To give one is to give them all. First, he wishes peace upon the disciples. Amid their fears and the bitterness accompanying their desertion of him, Jesus offers them peace. But this wish has a cost, for the second aspect is the disciples' responsibility to carry out Jesus' mission. He sends them, as the Father has sent him. The third aspect of this gift is the core of Christian mission. The disciples receive authority to forgive sins and to hold sins bound. They must exercise this authority wisely, and never apart from the Spirit. Most often, they must forgive. Since throughout John's gospel sin is synonymous with unbelief, this is another way of expressing the church's mission to proclaim Jesus.

The second half of today's gospel presents Thomas' doubts and his eventual recognition of Jesus. His words are the literary and theological climax of John's gospel, and of the New Testament: "My Lord and my God!" Jesus appears to rebuke him but he really offers an invitation to the whole world: Blessed are the ones who have not seen as Thomas as seen, and have yet believed.

Questions for Reflection

•How should Christians be responsible to and for one another? Why must Christians act responsibly toward the rest of the world? How can we do this? What is your share of the church's responsibilities?

•Imagine that you have joined the disciples in their hideout behind locked doors. What do you fear? What do you most expect Jesus to say, if he should speak to you?

•How do you receive Jesus' wish for peace? What role do you play in his mission?

•Whom must you forgive? How will you do it?

THIRD SUNDAY OF EASTER

Witness

[April 13, 1997; May 7, 2000; April 13, 2003]

First Reading: Acts 3:13–15, 17–19

God raised him from the dead, and we are his witnesses.

There are many speeches in the Acts of the Apostles. The first is Peter's Pentecost sermon, an exuberant, almost reckless public proclamation that results in mass baptisms. Today we read from the contrasting second speech, which follows Peter's healing of a cripple, and which leads to his arrest and confinement.

These words elaborate on a theme from the first speech. They are not designed to delight the Jerusalem authorities. Talking to a Jewish audience, Peter insists that God has glorified Jesus, whose execution they have engineered. He accuses them: "You put to death the Author of life. But God has raised him up." Acting ignorantly, like their leaders, these Israelites have fulfilled what God announced long ago. Peter also echoes John the Baptizer and Jesus: "Reform your lives, turn to God, so that your sins may be erased."

While the church has met early success, it has also encountered resistance. In both respects, the church follows Jesus' own path. It carries his message and offers freedom from afflictions and sin.

We must not overlook the core message: God raised him up. Too often Christians have neglected what matters most and vilified the Jews. But to bully someone else is to engage in mere thuggery, and to distort beyond recognition the message of the One who accuses no one, the One by whose standards we are all measured. Our business is to proclaim the Author of life, raised from the dead. We are his witnesses.

Responsorial Psalm: Psalm 4:2, 4, 7–8, 9

Second Reading: 1 John 2:1–5

He is an offering for our sins....

Fondly addressing "little ones," the author wants to keep them from sin. But even so, if anyone sins, Christ intercedes for us. He is an offering for all the sins of the world. This is a highly developed, late-first-century understanding of the resurrection.

Echoing John the evangelist, the author insists that knowing the

Lord is bound up with keeping his word/commandments. In turn, to keep his word is to manifest God's love made perfect in us.

Gospel: Luke 24:35–48

...he opened their minds....

In contrast to the abrupt ending of Matthew's gospel and Mark's non-ending, John and Luke tell several resurrection stories. Last week, we read John's version of Jesus' first appearance to apostles. Here we have Luke's account of a similar appearance.

Jesus stands in their midst and says, "Peace to you." They think they are seeing a ghost. He assures them, inviting them to touch the wounds, and their panic turns to joy. He asks them for something to eat and reminds them of his insistence that the law, the prophets, and the psalms have had to be fulfilled. Then he opens their minds to the Scriptures. He shows them that he is the messiah who has suffered and risen from the dead. To all nations the disciples must preach penance for the remission of sins. They are his witnesses.

Within a shared framework, Luke's emphasis differs from, even conflicts with, John's. Having described Jesus' appearance to two disciples on the road to Emmaus (24:13–35), Luke argues that Jesus has fulfilled the Scriptures. Here he does the same. Likewise, in both of Luke's stories, Jesus eats with the disciples. John emphasizes neither of these themes. Moreover, whereas in John's story the disciples recognize Jesus instantly, for Luke recognition comes more gradually.

What are we to make of these differences? It would be dishonest to force the two stories together into an uneasy harmony. Instead, we ought to read them as differing aspects of a reality too big to see from a single point of view. Luke portrays Jesus as healer, fulfiller, one who eats with us, whom we recognize gradually. John teaches that Jesus is unmistakably God among us. Both portraits are true. Each teaches an essential aspect of the mystery of the One who is risen. The tensions between them show us that no portrait of Jesus is adequate. Nothing can substitute for our own encounter with him.

Questions for Reflection

• When have you acted out of ignorance? What resulted from your action? How have you tried to change, to reform your life? What results have come from your efforts?

• How do you obey the Lord's commandments?

• How do you bear witness to the forgiveness of sins? How merciful are you?

Fourth Sunday of Easter

Good shepherd

[April 20, 1997; May 14, 2000; April 20, 2003]

First Reading: Acts 4:8–12

...this man stands before you perfectly sound.

After healing a cripple and preaching about Jesus, Peter has been arrested. Now facing the same priests responsible for the accusations leading to Jesus' crucifixion, he speaks boldly: "If we have to tell you why we dared to heal a cripple, then you too must answer for something. You crucified Jesus, whom God has raised from the dead. This man, once crippled, now stands before you in the power of Jesus' name. Jesus is the stone you rejected, and he is now the cornerstone [Psalm 118:2]. There is no salvation in anyone else."

Peter now Bold

Can this be the same Peter who once fled a similar scene? Now he is made sound in Jesus' name, like the man he has healed. Once a cripple full of blustery and empty promises, now he faces mortal danger without blinking.

This episode illustrates the tension that existed between Jews who believed in Jesus and those who did not. Eventually these tensions would prove irreconcilable, and Jews and Christians would go their separate ways. What matters most here is that Jesus heals all forms of infirmity and limitation. It is our job in all circumstances to bear witness to this most profound truth.

Responsorial Psalm: Psalm 118:1, 8–9, 21–23, 26, 29

Second Reading: 1 John 3:1–2

...we are God's children now.

Implying the presence of some form of persecution, the author explains why the world does not recognize us. The world never recognized the Son. We are his brothers and sisters. We have been made God's children by the grace of God's love. But there is more. We will become something else. It is not yet clear to us what we will become, but we will be like God, and will see God as God is.

Gospel: John 10:11–18

I am the good shepherd.

Jesus identifies himself as the good shepherd, evoking an image of God presented in Psalm 23 and elsewhere. He also explores the image: Unlike the hired hand, the shepherd lays down his life for the sheep. The one who works for pay runs at the first sight of the wolf, because he or she does not really care about the sheep.

Jesus also describes his care for the sheep. He knows them in the same way that he knows the Father and the Father knows him. He will give his life for them. Jesus must also lead other sheep who do not belong to this fold, so that they will hear his voice and there will be one flock. This image compares our relationship with Jesus to that of a parent and child in mutual embrace. Finally Jesus abandons the imagery and speaks plainly. He lays down his life freely. He has the power to lay it down and the power to take it up again.

This text is saturated with clues through which the church would later discern more explicit statements of revealed truth. Writing very late in the first century or early in the second, John writes for a church that has long been distinct from Judaism and that also seems to have differed significantly from other churches. Jesus' words about sheep belonging to another flock may refer to members of those other churches, or to Jews, or to pagans yet to hear the gospel. All will be brought into one flock, not only at the end, but also in earthly unity among the churches. Jesus' total identification with the Father is a foundation for the doctrine of the Trinity, spelled out some three centuries after the completion of John's account. His insistence that he can lay down his life and take it up again seems to refute Gnostic teachings that tended to question the incarnation. John's phrasing is a foretaste of the creed: true God from true God…he was born of the virgin Mary and was made man.

Questions for Reflection

•What are your biggest limitations? How have your choices and actions limited or even crippled you? How does Peter challenge you? How will you respond to his challenge?

•What work has God called you to do? What is your attitude toward your work? Do you act like the good shepherd, like a hired hand, or like someone in between? How can you improve the way in which you work?

•For what and for whom are you willing to lay down your life? How well do your actions, your choices, your motives reflect your principles? How well do they reflect the principles of the gospel?

FIFTH SUNDAY OF EASTER

The vine

[April 27, 1997; May 21, 2000; April 27, 2003]

First Reading: Acts 9:26–31

...the church was at peace.

Saul wishes to join the disciples in Jerusalem, but they fear him. After all, he has presided over the stoning of Stephen and harassed followers of Christ at every opportunity. But the trusted Barnabas commends him and testifies for Saul. The disciples take Saul in, and before long he runs afoul of some Greek-speaking Jews, who try to kill him. To save his life the disciples sneak him out to Tarsus. The church's most important theologian thus begins his career running for his life. This narrative adds extra drama to the story of Saul's encounter with Christ (Acts 9:1–19ff.). He who once persecuted Christians has now become just like them. Yet amid all the turmoil described here, Luke reminds us that the church is at peace, making steady progress and increasingly consoled by the Holy Spirit. In light of Saul's predicament, we can only assume that the church is at peace internally, while facing mortal danger from outside.

We should bear some things in mind. First, like the same author's companion book, the gospel of Luke, the Acts of the Apostles was written some fifty years after the events it narrates. The words "church," "Christians," "apostles," and "Jews" had come to connote precise distinctions by 85 C.E., when Luke wrote, but at the time of the events, these terms were meaningless; the first "Christians" were Jews who professed belief in Jesus Christ. The "church" mentioned in the early chapters of Acts consisted of groups of disciples, and their disciples, united by their belief in Jesus. The name "Christian" was originally an insult which meant literally "followers of the oily one" (*Messiah*="the anointed"=*Christos*).

In light of these things, Saul's change of heart looks less like a conversion and more like an embrace of a dynamic new movement within his professed religion. In his understanding, as in those of all leaders later called apostles (literally "ones who are sent"), mortal danger comes with the job. It is the path that Jesus has taken.

Responsorial Psalm: Psalm 22:26–27, 28, 30, 31–32

Second Reading: 1 John 3:18–24

…let us love in deed and in truth and not merely talk.

Addressing the audience as "little children," the author expounds on this letter's central theme. We must love, as we have been loved, in action that matters, and not just in talk. The quality of our love is a measure of our commitment to the truth and the strength of our belief. All other considerations are secondary: We must believe in Jesus and love one another as he has commanded us.

Gospel: John 15:1–8

I am the vine, you are the branches.

Jesus describes relationships among himself, the Father, and the disciples, with a most familiar image. Jesus is the true vine, and the Father is the vinegrower. We are the branches. Apart from him we can do nothing. If we "live in him" we produce abundantly, but if we do not "live in him" we wither, and we risk being thrown into the fire. If we live in him we may ask for anything. We have glorified the Father by bearing fruit, by becoming Jesus' disciples.

Like every other reference to vines in the four gospels, this must be understood in its Jewish context, in which the vine is Israel (see Isaiah 27:2–6; Jeremiah 2:21; 5:10; Hosea 10:1; Ezekiel 15:1–6; 17:5–10; 19:10–14; Psalm 80:8–15; and especially Isaiah 5:1–7). God is the vinegrower. But with these inflammatory words, John insists that Jesus has replaced Israel.

Keeping in mind that we must overcome the severe anti-Jewish character of much of John's gospel (see *Catechism of the Catholic Church*, 839), we can also savor the power of this imagery. A grapevine can grow wild to occupy great chunks of real estate. It is more useful when its branches submit to the discipline of the vinedresser. They can produce grapes but also leaves for nourishment, shade, and shelter, and fuel for warmth. Christ is the vine who has subjected himself to the Father's discipline, and we are branches.

Questions for Reflection

• What is peace? How is it more than, or different from, mere absence of violence? What does it take for a society to be at peace? What can you contribute to peace?

• What evidence suggests that you live as a branch on the vine that is Christ? What evidence suggests that some pruning is in order? What must you do?

SIXTH SUNDAY OF EASTER

Love one another

[May 4, 1997; May 28, 2000; May 4, 2003]

First Reading: Acts 10:25–26, 34–35, 44–48

God shows no partiality.

This text is the companion to the first reading of Easter Sunday's Mass. Together the two texts present the entire story of Peter at the home of the Roman centurion Cornelius. Today's reading outlines and concludes the visit. It resembles Luke's description of the first Christian Pentecost (Acts 2) in important ways: Prompted by the Spirit, Peter speaks to a crowd; the speech sketches principal Christian beliefs; the Spirit descends and is made evident in tongues; many are baptized.

But as important as the similarities are, there is one big difference, and a smaller, more subtle one. The big difference is that here for the first time Peter addresses a Gentile assembly, and finds them most receptive. He begins to understand that Christ is savior of all, and that the Spirit is available to all. The smaller difference is related. Whereas in previous sermons Peter has called for repentance (Acts 2:38ff.; 3:19ff.), here he reflects aloud upon the apostles' mission to preach forgiveness to all the world (10:42–43). This subtle difference is a turning point. It portrays Peter obeying what Luke narrates as Jesus' final charge to the church (Luke 24:44–48, echoed in Acts 1:8). The episode explains and justifies the beginning of the church's mission to the world.

Responsorial Psalm: Psalm 98:1, 2–3, 3–4

Second Reading: 1 John 4:7–10

Beloved, let us love one another.

This entire letter is like the musical form known as "theme and variations." The theme comes from the two great commandments (Matthew 22:34–40; Mark 12:28–31; Luke 10:25–28; see also Deuteronomy 6:5; Leviticus 19:18). The letter examines our various obligations to love God and love our neighbors.

These verses insist that our love for one another reveals whether we know God, whether we have been "begotten of God." The essence of love is God's initiative, not ours. God has loved us, offering the Son. Because God has loved us first, we are able to love.

Gospel: John 15:9–17

...love one another as I have loved you.

Having just illuminated the relationships among Father, Son, and disciples with vine imagery (John 15:1–8, fifth Sunday of Easter, year B), Jesus now speaks of our obligations. There is one principal demand: "You live in my love so long as you keep my commandments. Love one another as I have loved you, even if you have to lay down your life for your friends. You are no longer slaves, because now you know everything revealed to me. Bear fruit, as healthy branches of the vine. Love one another."

John the evangelist tends to speak in a cascade of images and assertions, because for him they are all connected. You cannot have one without the others. In his account, Jesus refers to himself as: source of living water (4:10ff.; 7:38); bread of life (6:35ff.); sent by the Father (e.g., 7:16); gate for the sheep (10:7ff.); good shepherd (10:11ff.); the resurrection and the life (11:25); light (12:46ff.); the way, the truth, and the life (14:6); advocate (14:16); true vine; and I AM (7:28, 58; 13:19; 18:5, 6, 8). All are true and necessary. You cannot have one without the others.

The demand that we love one another is part of Jesus' teaching about the vine. We are branches, subject to the vinegrower's discipline. It is one thing for us to decide for ourselves what love is, but to do so would be to run wild and to bear bad fruit. It is entirely another thing for us to learn to love as branches of the true vine, as drinkers of living water and eaters of bread of life, as sent by the One who has been sent, as sheep, and as followers of the way.

Questions for Reflection

• How well do you contribute to the church's mission of preaching forgiveness to the world? What can you do more effectively? What are you already doing well?

• What do you express in your actions? How do you express love to your family, your friends, to everyone else?

• How would your life change if starting today your every action reflected your willingness to lay down your life for your friends? What things would stay the same?

• How would our world change if starting today everyone obeyed Jesus' love command?

• What can you contribute, right now, to a world that obeys Christ's command to love?

ASCENSION OF OUR LORD

Message and signs

[May 8, 1997; June 1, 2000; May 8, 2003]

First Reading: Acts 1:1–11

...within a few days you will be baptized with the Holy Spirit.

Alone among the evangelists Luke has given us two volumes. Here are the opening verses of volume two. After again greeting Theophilus, Luke summarizes the first book, which deals with all that Jesus did and taught until he was taken up. He who had died appeared to his apostles many times during forty days to teach them about God's kingdom. He also told them to remain in Jerusalem until their baptism in the Holy Spirit.

Next Luke narrates the ascension a second time (see Luke 24:50–53). The apostles ask Jesus, "Are you going to restore the kingdom to Israel now?" and he diverts their attention. They will receive power when the Holy Spirit descends, he says, and they will witness to him throughout the earth. Then Jesus is lifted up from their sight.

The story concludes with two men dressed in dazzling garments posing a question to the apostles: "Why do you stand here looking up at the skies? Jesus will return." Their appearance parallels the appearance of two men who soften the terror of the women at the empty tomb (24:4–7). They, too, have asked a question: "Why do you seek the living one among the dead?"

The matter-of-fact tone suggests that extraordinary things do happen when God acts in our lives. In both encounters, the witnesses have been changed, and now they have work to do. The two men in dazzling clothes underline what Jesus has already taught: "You will receive the Spirit. You will announce the Good News to the world." Because they remind us of the messengers at the empty tomb, they also establish the purpose of Luke's second volume. The ascension interprets the resurrection, just as the men at the tomb have done. It offers the beginning of Luke's long answer to the question: Who reveals the presence of the risen Christ in the world?

Responsorial Psalm: Psalm 47:2–3, 6–7, 8–9

Second Reading: Ephesians 1:17–23

God has put all things under Christ's feet.

These verses hint at Christ's ascension: "...and seating him at his right hand in heaven." A similar hint appears in our creed. Christ's ascension was an important doctrine early in the life of the church. The author prays for an enlightening spirit of wisdom and insight for the converted pagans of Ephesus, for their recognition of the enormous power of God who has raised Jesus from the dead. The image of Christ's body describes the church in rich terms: The church is the fullness of the one who fills the universe. This statement is more a wish for what might be than a statement of fact. It holds us responsible to make things happen.

Gospel: Mark 16:15–20

...proclaim the good news to all creation.

These verses are universally recognized as the work of someone other than Mark. It is likely that they were written during the second century, possibly because the oldest existing manuscript ends abruptly (16:1–8). The author of these verses and the remainder of the so-called "longer ending" (16:9–20) seems to have been influenced by and to have restated portions of Luke 24 and John 20. Although since ancient times other possible endings have been known, the council of Trent declared this one inspired.

Jesus tells the eleven to proclaim the good news to all of creation. Whoever believes in and accepts the good news will be saved, but a bleaker fate awaits anyone who refuses to believe. Those who profess faith will be accompanied by signs: They will be able to expel demons, speak new languages, handle serpents, drink poison, and heal the sick.

Then Jesus is taken up into heaven, to be seated at God's right hand. The eleven obey Jesus' command to preach, and the Lord continues to work through them.

Questions for Reflection

•How do you contribute to the church's mission of announcing the good news to the world? What have you not yet done, that perhaps you should do?

•Why did the first-century church decide that Christians of all eras should know about Christ's ascension? Of all the things that could have been told about Jesus, why this? What does the ascension contribute to the ongoing life and ministry of the church?

•How does the Lord continue to work through the church? What signs suggest that he is with us?

SEVENTH SUNDAY OF EASTER
Doing the truth

[May 11, 1997; June 4, 2000; May 11, 2003]

First Reading: Acts 1:15–17, 20–26
...one...should be named as witness....

This episode at the beginning of the Acts of the Apostles is curious. Jesus has ascended to the Father (Acts 1:6–12, also Luke 24:50–52), and the disciples await the Holy Spirit. Of all possible things to do in this situation, why would they replace Judas? And why would they draw lots to choose Matthias? In Luke's understanding of Christian origins, twelve apostles are necessary, probably to accentuate the church as the "new Israel," with twelve leaders. Also, the lots draw attention to the Spirit's absence. All decisions made later in the narrative reflect discernment and the Spirit's power in the church. Not yet seeing the Spirit among them, the apostles revert to an ancient method of decision making (e.g., Joshua 18:6ff.) that pagans still practice at the crucifixion (e.g., Luke 23:34).

The most important term in this episode may be "witness to the resurrection." Whether an apostle is an eyewitness in our modern sense is unimportant. The Greek word translated here is literally "martyr," one whose life has been so transformed that he or she reveals the resurrected Christ. We are all invited to witness in this way.

Responsorial Psalm: Psalm 103:1–2, 11–12, 19–20

Second Reading: 1 John 4:11–16
God is love.

Here is more on God's love, and our love. The statement that no one has ever seen God seems to contradict much of what we read in the Hebrew Bible. After all, Abraham is said to have welcomed God to dinner (Genesis 18:1–5) and a story tells of Jacob wrestling with God (Genesis 32:23–31). But the author writes for a late first-century audience ignorant of the Hebrew tradition. Moreover, the author may wish to underline Christ's exclusive character as the One who reveals the Father.

the more we love, the more we experience God.

For us, too, the author's words speak a powerful truth. We have not seen God in the same way in which we see landscapes, plants, animals, one another, and the things we make. Yet if we love one another, we see the effects of God's love all around us. When we acknowledge the Son as savior, God dwells in us, and we in God.

Gospel: John 17:11–19
...they do not belong to the world.

John's entire chapter 17 describes the prayer with which Jesus concludes his teaching. These verses ask the Father's protection for those entrusted to him. They have been taken from their setting in John's account of the gospel and set into the church's year between the Ascension and Pentecost. It is easy to think of them as Jesus' prayer on behalf of the disciples awaiting the Spirit.

We ought also to hear these words as Jesus' prayer for us. We are descendants of the apostles. Everything we know about Jesus Christ comes from them. We have received their testimony, and we share their responsibilities. It is fair to say, therefore, that Jesus prays for us in this manner: May we share his joy. May we be consecrated by truth and in truth. May we who do not belong to the world yet go out into the world to speak and to do the truth.

Questions for Reflection
• Although no one has seen God in a literal sense, when have you seen God in other ways? How have you seen? Who helped you to see? Who helped you to determine that what you saw was really God?

• When and how do you help others to see God?

• How have you shared in Christ's joy? If you have not, why have you missed out?

• What evidence suggests that you have been consecrated in truth and by truth? What evidence might suggest something else?

• How do you speak the truth in the world? How do you do the truth? What can you do to satisfy more completely your responsibility to speaking and doing the truth?

PENTECOST

The body is one

[May 18, 1997; June 11, 2000; May 18, 2003]

First Reading: Acts 2:1–11

...each of us hears them speaking...about the marvels God has accomplished.
The Spirit graces our world and prompts us to build peace, justice, and
love, after Jesus' example. Christians recognized long ago that without
the Spirit we can do nothing. This article of faith pervades the books of
our New Testament

On the feast of the Torah, Pentecost, so named because it falls fifty
days after the Passover, Jews from all nations have made the pilgrim-
age to Jerusalem. Over the clamor of a great crowd, they hear a noise
like a strong, driving wind. Soon after this, they witness something
strange. Some Galileans speak, yet everyone can understand. To the
person in the crowd, the marvel is that each hears Peter and companions speaking in his and her native tongue.

Leading up to this first public act of the church after Jesus' ascension,
Luke's narrative has given us a peek into the room where the disciples
hide. When they hear the noise, tongues like fire rest on each of them.
They are filled with the Holy Spirit. They express themselves in foreign
tongues and make bold proclamation. They have seen Jesus risen from
the dead, but they also know that they are in peril. The real marvel is
that this is the same bunch who once deserted Jesus. Now, just a few
weeks after his execution, they burst into a multinational assortment of
people to announce Jesus' own good news.

Responsorial Psalm: Psalm 104:1, 24, 29–30, 31, 34

Second Reading: 1 Corinthians 12:3–7, 12–13

There are different gifts but the same Spirit.

Paul's first verse teaches that only in the Holy Spirit can anyone say
"Jesus is Lord." It seems to suggest that a person's ability to say particular words is evidence of the Holy Spirit. But Paul knows as well as you
and I do that anyone can speak words. History offers countless examples of proper words used improperly. Jesus seems to have insisted that
words alone mean nothing.

Paul understands that we say "Jesus is Lord" in words *and* in actions. Faithful actions have everything to do with Paul's understanding of unity-in-diversity. Most of the twelfth chapter of 1 Corinthians compares the various gifts in the church to the functions of different parts of the body. This text excerpts a few verses to represent the whole.

There are many gifts, but the same Spirit. We do different things, but for the same purpose, for the common good. There are many members in the body. We were all baptized in the one Spirit into the body that is Christ. Paul implies that when we use our gifts for the common good, we say with every fiber of our being, "Jesus is Lord." That is something we can only do in the Holy Spirit.

Gospel: John 20:19–23

Receive the Holy Spirit.

This text may contain the Bible's most important verses. Catholics proclaim them every year, twice: on the second Sunday of Easter and on Pentecost. We cannot hear these words too often, for they speak the deepest truth of our life. In this masterfully crafted story, Jesus fulfills the things that he has predicted. In his last discourse (14:1–16:33) he promised a peace that the world cannot give, and the constant assistance of the Holy Spirit. Here, appearing to the disciples for the first time after his resurrection, he gives them peace and the Holy Spirit.

He also gives two things that were not foretold. Now that the church has received the Spirit, he can teach things that had not been accessible before. Jesus gives the church a job: "As the Father has sent me, so I send you." He also gives a grave authority, that of forgiving sins or of holding them bound. Keeping in mind that for John sin is virtually synonymous with unbelief, we may understand that our job is to invite the world into faith on the day of Pentecost through credible word and action. We are the body of Christ. It is our job to give peace and forgiveness in the world. We could not do any of this, except in the Holy Spirit.

Questions for Reflection

• How can you offer genuine peace to others?

• What are five gifts with which you have been blessed? How can you use each in service of our shared Christian mission of peace and reconciliation?

• What would it cost you to become a better disciple than you are already? What could persuade you to pay this price?

TRINITY SUNDAY
(SUNDAY AFTER PENTECOST)
Father, Son, and Spirit

[May 25, 1997; June 18, 2000; May 25, 2003]

Sometimes the term "doctrinal feasts" is used to describe the first two Sundays after Pentecost and the Friday after the second Sunday (solemnity of the Sacred Heart). It refers to the fact that these and some other feasts celebrate truths revealed to the church after the last word of the Bible was written.

First Reading: Deuteronomy 4:32–34, 39–40
...the Lord is God...and there is no other.

At the entrance to the promised land, after forty years' testing in the wilderness, the chosen people pause to hear Moses speak. The book of Deuteronomy, written at least five centuries after the events it describes, cannot be read as a report of history. It is, however, a literary masterpiece. The author seizes a moment of high drama to set forth the essence of Jewish belief and practice. The book consists of sermons and invitations given by Israel's most revered teacher as the people stand poised to enter the land for which they have endured years of testing.

The introductory sermon summarizes and interprets the desert wanderings. It concludes with today's verses: "Did any other god," asks Moses, "ever do anything so great as what has been done for you? This is why you must know, and build into your hearts forever, that the Lord is God, in the heavens and on the earth. You must keep the law that I will teach you today, so that you and your children may prosper in the land given to you forever."

Responsorial Psalm: Psalm 33:4–5, 6, 9, 18–19, 20, 22

Second Reading: Romans 8:14–17
...we cry out, "Abba."

The fundamental Christian doctrine is the Trinity. Everything we teach and do is built upon this foundation. It shapes our professions of faith, our sacramental celebrations, and even the familiar ritual with which we open and close our prayers. Although the doctrine of the Trinity is not stated anywhere in the New Testament, these verses capture its essence. The mystery who is God is illuminated by the relationships God embraces, among the three persons of the Trinity, and with us.

The Spirit of God animates a people who can now call God "Abba," best translated as "Daddy." God's Spirit does not enslave. Rather, the Spirit frees us and adopts us. We are heirs, like Christ. We share in his sufferings, his glory, and his responsibilities.

Gospel: Matthew 28:16–20
...know that I am with you always....

Matthew's account of the gospel concludes with these verses. Summoned to a mountain in Galilee, the disciples see and recognize Jesus. All their remaining doubts are driven away. Exercising the authority that has created and sustained the world, Jesus tells them to go and make disciples of all the nations and to baptize them in the name of the Father and of the Son and of the Holy Spirit.

This baptismal formula assures us that even though the doctrine of the Trinity is not stated formally in the New Testament, Matthew certainly seems to have written with something very much like it in mind. And since Matthew's choice of words reflects realities known to his first-century church, we can be confident that long before the doctrine was stated, still it served as a foundation for the church's life.

Today we are Jesus' disciples, and we carry the same responsibility as those whom Matthew portrays bowing before Jesus on a Galilee mountaintop. We must go out to the world, baptize the world, and teach the world to carry out everything Jesus has commanded. Such a job would be impossible, except that Jesus is with us, always.

Questions for Reflection

• What great things has God done for you? What other god or gods sometimes tempt you to overlook what God has done? How do you handle temptation?

• How have you experienced God as Father, as "Daddy"? When has God touched you as equal, as brother or sister? How often do you live in *koinonia*, the fellowship of the Holy Spirit that binds you with others in a common life?

• Why do we baptize in the name of the Father and of the Son and of the Holy Spirit? Why don't we just baptize in the name of Jesus?

FEAST OF CORPUS CHRISTI
(BODY AND BLOOD OF CHRIST)
Nourishment and challenge

[June 1, 1997; June 25, 2000; June 1, 2003]
[Following this day, in 1997 and 2003 proceed to tenth Sunday in ordinary time,
p. 100. In 2000 proceed to thirteenth Sunday in ordinary time, p. 106.]

First Reading: Exodus 24:3–8
This is the blood of the covenant.

Well into the desert wanderings, after the mysterious encounter at Mt. Sinai, Moses has given structure to Israelite life. He has given to the people the law that he has received from God, including the ten commandments. Here, the people respond: "We will do everything that the Lord has told us."

Moses writes down all of God's words and builds an altar among twelve pillars representing the tribes. Then, having directed the sacrifice of young bulls, he pours half the blood on the altar. Reading the covenant aloud, he sprinkles the remaining blood on the people.

The ancient covenant is an agreement, entered freely by both sides, supported by and symbolizing a powerful historical relationship. It is sealed with a ritual intended to remain vivid in the memory of the people.

Today our rituals are tidier and considerably more polite than Moses' bull-blood poured on altar and people. Our rituals remind us of, and celebrate, our commitments and our continued wanderings in a world that often looks like a wilderness and in which God sometimes seems more absent than present. Our most important ritual, the Eucharist, celebrates the unique sacrifice of Christ, God's covenant of enduring presence with us.

Responsorial Psalm: Psalm 116:12–13, 15–16, 17–18

Second Reading: Hebrews 9:11–15
...his death has taken place for deliverance....

Christ's covenant is contrasted with the first covenant in terms that, frankly, do little justice to first-century Jewish understandings. The author describes the first covenant as a cleansing enacted annually with the blood of animals. It was and is much more than that. For Jews, then and today, the covenant is a reminder and celebration of the exodus, the wanderings, and the social organization and ethical commitments directed by God.

Even so, the blood of Christ cleanses. Whether the letter is addressed to Jews or to a universal audience, it appeals to our desire for an eternal inheritance. No matter who we are, Christ's sacrifice has cleansed us so that we might worship the living God.

Gospel: Mark 14:12–16, 22–26
...this is my body...this is my blood....

These verses cover ground similar to that to the epistle, but in narrative form. Taken from Mark's account of the passion, they describe arrangements for the Passover meal and the most important part of the last supper. At table with the disciples, Jesus takes bread, blesses it, and gives it to them, saying, "This is my body." Repeating these gestures with a cup, he tells them, "This is my blood. It is the blood of the covenant, poured out for many. I will drink it again only in the reign of God."

Although today our rites may be tidy, the realities they celebrate are not. We who are accustomed to weekly, even daily, Eucharist can too easily lose sight of its origins. The Eucharist is not a polite thing. It reminds us of a brutal injustice that God has turned into the greatest of all triumphs. The Eucharist is therefore our hope, in even the most terrible situations. When we eat this bread and drink this cup, we enter into the cross and glorification of Jesus. We are cleansed and renewed and nourished. But we also do more than receive. We commit ourselves anew to wandering with God, and to all the responsibilities bound up in that wandering. We too are the body of Christ, a sign of his presence in and for the world.

Questions for Reflection

•In what ways do you think the Eucharist specifically nourishes you? How does it challenge you? How does the Eucharist nourish the church? How does it challenge? What does it require that we do?

•What brutalities or injustices afflict you? How does the Eucharist sustain you in the face of these things? What brutalities or injustices plague your household, your neighborhood, your town, our world? What difference does the Eucharist make? What can you do to make things better?

•How easy is it for you just to wander with God? What tends to keep you from wandering?

SECOND SUNDAY IN ORDINARY TIME

Come and see

[*January 19, 1997; January 16, 2000; January 19, 2003*]

For more than half of the church year, we dwell in "ordinary time." Unlike the Sundays of Advent, Christmas, Lent, and Easter, all of which focus on particular aspects of the mystery of Christ, Sundays in ordinary time celebrate the mystery more generally.

The thirty-three or thirty-four Sundays of ordinary time occupy two sections of the year. The first extends from the feast of the Baptism of the Lord to Ash Wednesday. In effect, it replaces what was called the "season of Epiphany" before the reforms of Vatican Council II. The second section begins on the Monday after Pentecost and concludes with the first Sunday of Advent.

First Reading: 1 Samuel 3:3–10, 19
...your servant is listening.

At the dawn of Israel's national history, when the ark is housed in a tent at Shiloh, Eli is priest and caretaker. The boy Samuel, fulfillment of a divine promise to his once-barren mother, has been dedicated to the Lord and lives with Eli. The boy awakens three times, and Eli understands the ritual significance: The Lord is calling Samuel.

At Eli's instruction the boy listens to God. In verses excluded from this reading, he learns of God's outrage towards, and curse upon, the wicked sons of Eli. In an abrupt conclusion to the reading, Samuel grows up powerful, embraced in the Lord's presence.

Responsorial Psalm: Psalm 40:2, 4, 7–8, 8–9, 10

Second Reading: 1 Corinthians 6:13–15, 17–20
...glorify God in your body.

In the seaport town of Corinth, some of the newly baptized Christians have failed to understand their freedoms. Seaports have always been wide-open places, it seems, and some Christians have assumed that their baptisms permit business as usual. Forcefully, Paul corrects them. The body is not for immorality, but for the Lord. Your bodies are members of Christ's mystical body. Sexual license is a sin against your own body, which is nothing less than a temple of the Holy Spirit. You do not belong to yourself, but to Christ; therefore, conduct yourself to glorify God.

Gospel: John 1:35–42
What are you looking for?

During this year we read from John occasionally to augment Mark's very short account of the gospel. Here, two of the Baptizer's disciples walk behind Jesus, who turns and asks, "What are you looking for?" Curious about his lodging, these disciples accept Jesus' invitation to "Come and see." One of them, Andrew, brings his brother Simon to Jesus, who names him Cephas, which means "head" in Greek. And as the evangelist explains, this man is also known as Peter, after the Latin word for "rock."

There is literary genius at work here. John has set the first words of Jesus after a prologue that resembles a Greek chorus and an opening scene in which the charismatic Baptizer proclaims the approach of the one who is truly great. These devices invite us into the drama. When we tag along behind Jesus, he asks us, "What are you looking for?" And he invites us, "Come and see." In all the rest of the gospel, throughout the year, and at every moment in our lives, Jesus asks us this same question: What are you looking for? Most people answer only partially, or inadequately, like the Baptizer's disciples who can only think of asking about where Jesus is staying. We devote even long lifetimes to answering again and again Jesus' question. What are you looking for? To every one of our honest-if-partial answers Jesus invites us: Come and see.

Questions for Reflection

•When and how have you heard what seems to have been God calling you? How can you determine whether God really is calling? What helps you to clarify matters? Whose help do you need?

•How well do you maintain your body, the temple of the Spirit? What changes should you make, if any?

•How do you answer Jesus' question today? What are you looking for?

•How recently have you accepted Jesus' invitation to come and see? Where has his invitation led you? What have you seen? Whether you have accepted this invitation recently or not, what clues does the gospel give you? Where does his invitation lead? What does it reveal to anyone who follows?

THIRD SUNDAY IN ORDINARY TIME

God calls us

[January 26, 1997; January 23, 2000; January 26, 2003]

First Reading: Jonah 3:1–5, 10

Set out for the great city of Nineveh....

These verses invite us into the book of Jonah. The world of this brief masterpiece is a world turned inside out. In Jonah's world the prophet runs from God's call, and alien sailors are more impressed with God's power than is God's own prophet. The king of a feared enemy repents immediately upon hearing of Jonah's God's displeasure. The prophet seems to want only to avoid personal discomfort, and when confronted by his maker, he rationalizes his pettiness. He never does understand that God's will is far more important than his own. The narrative is wholly preposterous, but the book is not. It is a satire that makes a serious point.

Today's verses place Jonah at last at Nineveh. Having fled and been thrown overboard, he has been swallowed by a fish and vomited onto shore. At the capital of the cruelest and most violent of Israel's enemies, he delivers his message. The whole city repents. No prophet before or since has ever enjoyed this kind of success. The final verse accentuates the book's main theme: God is not constrained by our senses of propriety or justice. God's mercy is incomprehensible, as is God's power. Even in the most impossible situations, and even through reluctant, buffoonish messengers, God forgives and gives life.

Responsorial Psalm: Psalm 25:4–5, 6–7, 8–9

Second Reading: 1 Corinthians 7:29–31

...the world as we know it is passing away....

One of Paul's most important convictions is that Christ's resurrection is the climax of human history. A consequence of this belief is his apparent endorsement of bachelorhood, an expression of his confidence that the final chapter of history will be over soon.

We know that the world has endured for two millennia beyond Paul's expectation. Even so, we can learn from the detachment he encourages in these verses. We must live as though we neither wept nor rejoiced, as though we owned nothing, leaving light footprints on the world.

Gospel: Mark 1:14–20

The reign of God is at hand!

After warding off the tempter in the wilderness, and following John's arrest, Jesus appears in Galilee. He wastes no time, proclaiming a message that includes that of the Baptizer and a good deal more. He announces the time of fulfillment, the reign of God, and his demand for personal reform and belief in the good news. He then begins to call together a group of disciples. Simon and Andrew are first, then James and John. All drop their nets, their livelihood, indeed their very lives, to come after him.

Their response to the divine call contrasts with that of Jonah. In the person of Jesus, God's servant embarks on a career that will culminate in a brutal, painful execution. In the persons of the disciples, God's servants abandon everything familiar in order to do Jesus' bidding. Here they act more like the dreaded king of Nineveh than like Jonah.

But when we recall the manner in which the rest of Mark's account portrays the disciples, we can see that they are quite like Jonah. While here they appear to do what is virtuous if risky, before long they look stupid and selfish. When the real costs of discipleship become apparent, these same disciples just cannot put enough distance between themselves and Jesus.

We are their descendants. Our faith is the faith that these original followers received from Jesus and handed over to us in the Scriptures and in the church's growing tradition. We have it within ourselves to follow Jesus, even as Jesus himself has followed the path onto which he has been called. We are also capable of running from our call and making excuses. The choice is ours. God's word, given to us, bears a power that we should never underestimate. Discipleship demands everything from us.

Questions for Reflection

•When did you run from something that God appeared to want you to do? What was the result? What have you done willingly in response to God's call? What resulted from your more faithful response?

•How has God been merciful to you? How does God show mercy to the world?

•When and how has God seemed to act through you, in spite of yourself?

• What, if anything, are you not willing to give up to follow Jesus? What keeps you from letting go?

FOURTH SUNDAY IN ORDINARY TIME

Prophets

[January 30, 2000;
Replaced by the Presentation of the Lord, 1997 and 2003, see page 150.]

First Reading: Deuteronomy 18:15–20

I will raise up for them a prophet like you....

Unlike many books in the collection that we call the Old Testament, the book of Deuteronomy exhibits a consistent style and narrative flow. This fact stands out among other evidence that leads modern scholars to conclude that it is much newer than many other books. Portions of the book were composed as the culmination of the reform movement instigated by King Josiah of Judah. These were added to other material during and soon after the exile. This "second law" (*deuteronomion*) is a masterful summation and interpretation of essentials.

Today's reading describes the job of the prophet. He or she is a leader like Moses. The prophet is raised up from among the people, and has no choice but to speak the words that God places in his or her mouth. It is implied that the prophet must act on behalf of the people, often before hostile powers, and sometimes before the people's own hostility. But our God is unlike any other god, and God's word is often hard to hear. Even Moses spoke and acted in error more than once. The prophet must listen for God's voice in the history of the people, as well as in natural signs and in extraordinary experiences.

Responsorial Psalm: Psalm 95:1–2, 6–7, 7–9

Second Reading: 1 Corinthians 7:32–35

I should like you to be free of all worries.

These verses could appear to prefer celibacy over marriage, but we must read them in context. Utterly convinced that Christ would return during or soon after his lifetime, Paul has little use for any human attachments. Also, Corinth is a wide-open seaport town, a place where anything goes. The apostle speaks to a sophisticated audience with reasoning, but also sometimes as a parent speaks to a small child. "It is for your own good," says Paul, "that you avoid any attachment that could divert your attention from the Lord." Married or celibate, we could all profit from this advice.

Gospel: Mark 1:21–28
Be quiet! Come out of the man!

In the company of his freshly called disciples, Jesus enters the synagogue at Capernaum on the sabbath and begins to teach. The people are spellbound (literally overcome with astonishment) with his teaching, for, unlike their scribes, Jesus teaches with authority.

Thus Mark introduces Jesus' public ministry. This introduction is loaded with tensions and conflicts that are, and only can be, resolved in the cross. Jesus teaches, for example, and he does the work of healing on the day of rest, in violation of the law. He is compared favorably with the scribes, the designated teachers of the time, and persons who eventually conspire against him.

The encounter with the man possessed by an unclean spirit provides a commentary on Jesus as teacher. The evil spirit recognizes him and confers upon him the name of the Holy One of God. That is a shocking pronouncement, for only the God of Israel is ever, under any circumstances, to be addressed as the Holy One.

Jesus commands the spirit, and it leaves the man immediately. The crowd remains amazed, because Jesus' teaching bursts the bounds of words and achieves immediate effect, just like the words of the Holy One at the dawn of creation (Genesis 1:1–2:4a). Probably without knowing it, the people find themselves in the presence of God. They are duly impressed, and they spread his reputation through all of Galilee.

Questions for Reflection
•Who is a prophet today? According to the prophet's job description listed in the comment about the first reading, who seems to be a prophet?

•Why do you think the Bible presents many different, and sometimes conflicting, descriptions of prophets?

•What are your attachments? What situations, things, or relationships absorb your best energies? When do your attachments get in the way of your devotion to Jesus?

•How can we recognize teaching that is authentic?

•What unclean spirits live in you? What can you do about them? Whom do you ask for help? How do you ask for help?

FIFTH SUNDAY IN ORDINARY TIME
The gospel

[February 9, 1997; February 6, 2000; February 9, 2003]

First Reading: Job 7:1–4, 6–7
Is not man's life on earth a drudgery?

On a wager, the Lord has allowed the Adversary to take away Job's wealth and his family, and then to afflict him with a horrible skin disease. Thus the question that dominates the drama of the entire book: Will Job curse God for his suffering, or not?

The book of Job is a literary masterpiece that embellishes an ancient folk tale, committed to writing by Ezekiel (14:12–20). The book's action is narrated at the beginning and the end (1:1–22; 42:11–17). In between, the dialogs between Job and his friends constitute what has been called the longest surviving Hebrew poem. The book brings together narrative and poetry, courtroom drama and lament, to explore the mystery of suffering in the lives of the just.

In today's verses Job has hit bottom. He complains, first about suffering in general, then about his own lot. "Life is a drudgery. We are all slaves panting for the reliefs promised by shade and higher wages. But there is no relief for me. My nights are sleepless and my days are hopeless. I shall never be happy again."

Why do people suffer? Why do bad things happen to good people? One response to these questions insists that suffering is punishment for wrongdoing. But the book of Job is too wise to settle for such a naive answer, or indeed for any answer. Suffering is a mystery. The person of faith can find God in all facets of life, even in suffering.

Responsorial Psalm: Psalm 147:1–2, 3–4, 5–6

Second Reading: 1 Corinthians 9:16–19, 22–23
I am ruined if I do not preach it!

Paul speaks of the gospel as a force that imposes itself upon the disciple, compelling him or her to speak. Like the prophets of old, the disciple has no choice but to preach. It is better to preach willingly than to do so against one's will. Having decided to preach willingly, Paul is free to adopt many roles: "I have made myself all things to all men in order to save at least some."

It is only in a secondary sense that it is proper to speak of "gospel" as a book. The accounts of Matthew, Mark, Luke, and John reflect portions of the larger reality of which Paul speaks. The gospel has remained alive and potent through all of the history of the church. The church has produced and promulgated the four books called "gospels." And in a continually growing Tradition the church continues to seek ways of proclaiming the gospel in all ages and circumstances.

Gospel: Mark 1:29–39

Let us move on....

Jesus' world is populated with human persons, but also with demons, assorted powers, and, most ominously, the Adversary. Today's first reading illustrates the psychological and emotional toll exacted by some of these unseen forces. The gospel text manifests Jesus' effortless authority over them all. First, he relieves Simon's mother-in-law of her fever. Her recovery is complete and instant, and she waits on those seated at the table. By the end of that same day, Jesus is set upon to expel demons from people suffering all manner of afflictions.

Jesus withdraws and the disciples literally hunt him down: The Greek verb connotes pursuit of an animal. Found, Jesus tells the apostles that they must move on to the next town, to do God's work. From this point on, Jesus almost never has a moment's peace, as he preaches the good news (the gospel) and expels demons in all of Galilee.

We moderns may think ourselves too sophisticated to talk about demons and other unseen powers. Our technological achievements tempt us to regard our ancestors as naive. Yet faith begins in our encounter with mystery, and there are many questions that technological know-how can never answer. Maybe there are and will remain unseen powers that affect us. Jesus holds mastery over all the powers that inhabit our world.

Questions for Reflection

•How have you suffered? Who has suffered in a way that commands your attention? How have you tried to relieve suffering, in your own or in someone else's life?

•How does the gospel impose itself upon you? What does the gospel demand that you do?

•How can Paul make himself all things to all people? How can anyone do this and keep his or her integrity?

•Why does Jesus both preach and expel demons? What do the two activities have in common?

Sixth Sunday in Ordinary Time

The one who heals

[February 13, 2000;
omitted 1997 and 2003. Proceed to first Sunday of Lent, p. 32.]

First Reading: Leviticus 13:1–2, 44–46

...the priest shall declare him unclean....

Among the many (613) laws given to Moses and recorded in the books of Exodus, Leviticus, Numbers, and Deuteronomy are these that deal with leprosy. The church has chosen them to illuminate an aspect of today's gospel text.

To the ancients, the term "leprosy" included what scientists today recognize as an infectious skin disease caused by bacteria, which eats away at skin and nerves. But long ago people knew nothing of bacteria, or of any means of controlling their spread. They only knew that contact with persons who had skin blemishes often spread those blemishes, and that sometimes those blemishes led to severe debilitation and death. To them, any visible skin disease was leprosy. Diseases we know today as psoriasis and dermatitis, for example, and chicken pox, smallpox, measles, and possibly even acne came under this heading. Many of these afflictions were contagious, and some could kill. Therefore many ancient people quarantined their "lepers."

In the Mosaic law the priest was responsible for public health. He would determine whether an afflicted person was a leper, to be declared "unclean." According to the law, a leper had to dress distinctively and to live apart from other people. While traveling from place to place he or she had to shout "unclean," in order to give others fair warning.

Responsorial Psalm: Psalm 31:1–2, 5, 11

Second Reading: 1 Corinthians 10:31–11:1

...you should do all for the glory of God.

Throughout his letters, Paul responds to the questions and pastoral concerns of local churches. These verses come from his extended discussion of what Christians ought to do about meat sacrificed to idols. While it is unlikely that we might worry about such a thing today, these verses are of special interest to us because they develop universal principles. They provide a fine example of the way in which Paul's mind works. In so doing they offer an insight into the rest of his thought, which in turn underpins most of the New Testament and the origins of Christian theology.

Whether we eat or drink, and whatever we do, we must desire to do everything for the glory of God. Having said that, we must also avoid offending or causing scandal to others, whether they be Jews or Gentiles or members of the church. We are responsible to others, just as we are responsible for ourselves. In meeting our responsibilities toward others, we act on behalf of God's glory.

Gospel: Mark 1:40–45
I will do it. Be cured.

Mark's first chapter sets a rapid pace. Jesus is baptized by John, and he fends off the tempter in the wilderness. He emerges into society after forty days and announces the reign of God while calling his disciples. His teaching and healings so impress people that he must move from town to town to escape the press of the crowd.

Here, at the end of the chapter, a leper violates prescribed behavior and approaches Jesus with a request for healing. Jesus complies and warns him not to tell anyone. Instead, the man should obey the ancient law of Moses by presenting himself to the priest and offering what is required. But the man makes the story public, and now Jesus can no longer enter a town openly. Staying in desert places, he yet finds people coming at him from all sides, hunting him down as though he were an animal.

With the story of the leper, Mark has completed his introduction of Jesus. The one whom the reader recognizes as the Son of God carries the good news of God's reign, in word and healing and action. But as the good news liberates others, its very success presses in upon the messenger and spares him not a moment's rest.

Questions for Reflection

• Who are today's lepers? Whom does our society banish to the margins of existence? Who is feared in our culture? What does Jesus' response to the leper ask of you, and the rest of the church?

• How can you give glory to God, in everything you do? What changes do you have to make, if any?

• When did you last have too many demands on your time and energy? How did you feel in this situation? What did you do for relief? What kept you going? How did you keep your priorities straight?

SEVENTH SUNDAY IN ORDINARY TIME

Something new

[omitted 1997; February 20, 2000; omitted 2003]

First Reading: Isaiah 43:18–19, 12–22, 24–25

...I am doing something new!

Even though several verses have been omitted from a portion of a poem of "Second Isaiah," this text still reads well. The poem, one of the songs of the servant of the Lord, interprets the exile endured by the Jews. The people have ignored their God, who has at last found their sins and their crime intolerable. The trial is over (see Isaiah 40:1–2), and God has now decided, for God's own sake, to erase the people's sins. The focus of this text is verse 19: "I am doing something new!" While the past is important, God can always make a fresh start. The poet urges us to discern God's will in our history and in our opportunities.

Responsorial Psalm: Psalm 41:2–3, 4–5, 13–14

Second Reading: 2 Corinthians 1:18–22

Whatever promises God has made have been fulfilled in him....

God always keeps the divine word. In this text, Paul invites the church at Corinth to look carefully at his words and example, to discover therein a consistency that resembles God's own. It is a daring comparison, but Paul claims no virtue for himself. He is convinced that Jesus Christ is never a "no," but rather always a "yes." He intends this word game as a metaphor. If God's word is fulfilled, then God's "yes," expressed most clearly in Christ, pervades the world and our lives. Paul's preaching, and that of his companions, has been focused on this conviction. If we are to say "yes" to God, we must respond "Amen" to God's most clear "yes," the word pronounced in the person of Jesus.

A banking metaphor suggests that an even more clear "yes" has yet to be pronounced. Christ has anointed and sealed us, and in so doing he has deposited the Spirit, the "first payment," in our hearts. Everything is to be understood in terms of Christ, but more remains to be understood.

Gospel: Mark 2:1–12

...your sins are forgiven.

Following an action-packed first chapter, Mark's account of the gospel shows Jesus taking a brief rest. It is then reported that Jesus is in Capernaum, and rapidly he is surrounded by a standing-room-only crowd. A paralytic is brought to him, lowered through the roof of the place where he is talking. This detail shows us that people will go to enormous lengths to seek his assistance. Viewing the paralyzed man and recognizing the faith of those who have brought him, Jesus announces that the man's sins are forgiven. Mindful of tradition, exemplified by today's first reading (and see Psalm 103:3, for example), some scribes in the crowd are indignant, for only God can forgive sin.

Jesus responds to their unspoken difficulties: "Which is easier, to tell the paralytic that his sins are forgiven, or to tell him to walk?" The scribes have no answer. Jesus declares his purpose, which is to establish the "Son of man's" authority to forgive sins. At his command, the paralytic walks. Echoing precisely the reaction of the synagogue crowd described in Mark 1:27 (fourth Sunday in ordinary time) the scribes and the others present marvel: "We have never seen anything like this."

It seems likely that Mark has tailored this story with today's first reading in mind. By resisting innovation, the scribes are to some extent, only doing their jobs, for they must preserve tradition. Before their very eyes, however, Jesus introduces a marvel of living tradition. Everything they know invites them to acknowledge that God is in fact doing something new. This is a vital question for Mark, for the scribes, and for us: How well do we allow God to do something new?

Questions for Reflection

•How do you think God has acted in your life? What new opportunities does God seem to set before you? How has God acted in history? What are the major events that our tradition has taught? What new things does God seem to be doing now? What opportunities does God set before the church and the world today?

•What difference does it make that Jesus is always "yes"? How often do you respond "Amen"? What must you do to respond more faithfully to all that Jesus has done for you and for the world?

•How do you strike a balance between the two essential forces, tradition and the new? How easy is it for you to accept or to do something new? How does the church strike its balance? God is doing something new: How do you respond?

Eighth Sunday in Ordinary Time

New wineskins

[omitted 1997; February 27, 2000; omitted 2003]

First Reading: Hosea 2:16, 17, 21–22

...you will know the Lord.

The brief book of Hosea is dominated by a single image comparing God's relationship with the chosen people to a marriage. The first chapter sets the stage for today's text. Hosea marries, but the union barely deserves the name. His wife, Gomer, conceives three children, and Hosea is father to none of them.

Hosea responds to Gomer's waywardness as God responds to the people: "I will court her in the desert, as in the old days, and she will respond eagerly." We are invited to recall the heated first blush of love, which is never bland or tidy, but always passionate. And we witness the prophet's hope, which is also God's hope: "We will be faithful and we will know one another completely, we will be together forever, in right and justice, love and mercy."

It may disturb us to think in these terms, but the imagery is quite plain: God demands a passionate intimacy with the chosen. To respond in kind we must do right and justice, love and mercy.

Responsorial Psalm: Psalm 103:1–2, 3–4, 8, 10, 12–13

Second Reading: 2 Corinthians 3:1–6

Our sole credit is from God....

Apparently responding to a request for a letter of recommendation, Paul condenses several images from the Jewish Bible. "You are our letter of recommendation," he says. "Anyone desiring our credentials should look at you. Here is what they will see: Our recommendation is written upon your hearts [Jeremiah 31:33], not on tablets of stone [Exodus 31:18; 32:15; Deuteronomy 9:10] but on tablets of human hearts [Ezekiel 11:19; Proverbs 7:3]."

Gospel: Mark 2:18–22

...new wine is poured into new skins.

Without a chance to catch his breath, Jesus has healed a paralytic lowered to him through a roof, has taught by the sea, and called a tax-collector to follow him. He has also sat at table with people worse than tax-collectors, the scum of the earth. Hearing of Jesus' reputation for partying, John's disciples and some Pharisees ask Jesus, "Why do we fast, and your disciples do not?" Jesus responds with three images: Guests do not fast in the company of the groom; no one sews unshrunken cloth on an old cloak; no one pours new wine into old wineskins.

The church seems to have linked the first reading with this text through the groom imagery. We must not be too quick to identify the bride, however, because since it is not Mark's concern he has given us no evidence with which to name her. On the other hand he does identify the guests with Jesus' associates. While the groom is with them, they must party. There will be time for fasting.

The remaining images speak common sense. To sew unshrunken cloth over a hole in an old garment is to frustrate your purpose. Before long, such a patch will tear away and make matters worse. Likewise, to pour new wine into hides that have already been stretched to their limits is to watch helplessly as the liquid ferments, their gasses expand, and the fruit of your labor spills and soaks the ground.

Jesus' answer to the Pharisees and John's disciples insists that something new is happening before their eyes, and that the new cannot be imposed on the old. In some ways it is a radical departure from the familiar. Jesus announces something new, the kingdom of God. It is manifest in his actions and in his words (Mark 1:21–28, fourth Sunday in ordinary time; Mark 1:40–45, sixth Sunday in ordinary time; Mark 2:1–12, seventh Sunday in ordinary time). Much of the old simply cannot accommodate the new.

Questions for Reflection

•Why does the prophet insist that right and justice, love and mercy belong together? How does God expect us to respond to God's faithfulness? Why is it necessary that we do justice and mercy, in particular?

•Who are your friends? With whom do you associate? How much time do you spend with people who are misfits, losers, "uncool"? With whom does Jesus associate? How does his example challenge or affirm your choices and your motivations?

•When is it appropriate to party? When is it appropriate to fast? How do you balance the two?

•In what ways does Christ seem to offer you new wine? How do you respond? What are your old wineskins? How do you make new ones?

NINTH SUNDAY IN ORDINARY TIME

Our duty

[omitted 1997; March 5, 2000; omitted 2003]

First Reading: Deuteronomy 5:12–15

The Jewish Bible recites the decalogue (ten commandments) in two places, Exodus 20:2–17 and Deuteronomy 5:6–21. The two texts are nearly identical, but for one detail reported in verse 15 of today's text: The people must not forget that they were freed from slavery by God's strong arm. That is why the sabbath must be observed.

Most scholars agree that parts of Deuteronomy were composed five centuries after the events it portrays, beginning during the reforms of Judah's king Josiah (2 Kings 22:8ff.). By contrast, portions of Exodus are much older, although these too were written between two and five centuries after events they relate. Moreover, the book of Exodus probably did not attain its final shape until during or immediately after the exile, a century after Deuteronomy was written. We can assume that the person or persons who collected and arranged the various writings into what would be called the Torah (see Nehemiah 8:1–12, third Sunday in ordinary time, year C) recognized the subtle difference between the two readings of the decalogue, and included it for a purpose.

It is clear that kingdom-wide ethical and moral improvements were expected. Deuteronomy 5:15 reminds its audience that compassion is not only a good thing to do. It is also the very reason for their existence. It is therefore an absolute, something the people must do. To meet the most basic of their duties, which is to observe the sabbath, the people must act compassionately, remembering their solidarity even with slaves.

Responsorial Psalm: Psalm 81:3–4, 5–6, 6–8, 10–11

Second Reading: 2 Corinthians 4:6–11

God...has shone in our hearts.

The disciple bears a stubborn, unquenchable light within a fragile earthen vessel. Paul has taken two metaphors and done something that a modern English teacher would discourage. It appears that he has mixed metaphors. Even so, the result is powerful, not at all clumsy. The disciple's purpose is defined by God's light shining on and glorifying Christ's face. Imagine that light contained in a clay urn. You may abuse the urn, chip away at it, and slowly the light will grow more apparent to you. If you break the urn, you see the light overpowering any darkness.

Paul regards his afflictions in a detached manner. We are afflicted in every way, full of doubts, persecuted, struck down. Our suffering only reveals Jesus' life, in our mortal flesh. Throughout, Paul never encourages suffering—or any experience—for its own sake, nor for any purpose that we might choose. Such behavior would be idolatry. On the other hand, if our purpose is genuinely defined by Christ's glorious example, then everything that happens to us reveals his light.

Gospel: Mark 2:23–3:6
Is it permissible to do a good deed on the sabbath...?
This text is rich with references to Hebrew tradition. Pharisees observe Jesus and the disciples picking grain on the sabbath, and they protest. Jesus meets them on their own terms, citing as precedent David's use of holy bread when he and his band were hungry (1 Samuel 21:1–7). In one pithy response he has not only appealed to the memory of Israel's legendary king, he has also drawn battle lines. Jesus continues with a nuanced understanding of the sabbath: It was made for us. We were not made for the sabbath.

Then he marches into the synagogue and points out a man with a shriveled hand. He poses an ethical question for the legal experts: Which is lawful, to do good or to do evil on the sabbath? He implies that it is evil to do nothing if you are able to do good. The experts refuse to answer, and Jesus knows that they have closed their minds against him. He heals the man, winning this battle on the very terms defined by those who have challenged him. And for their part, they plot with others to defeat him on other, more violent terms.

Questions for Reflection
•What is your most basic religious duty? How do you try to fulfill it? How often have the needs of others seemed to be in tension with your religious duty? How do you resolve this tension?

•How have you suffered? How do you deal with your suffering?

•Underneath everything else, what seems to be your purpose? How did you discover it? Who seems to have defined your purpose?

•What good can you do? How do you do it? How often do you fail to perform whatever good you are able to do? How do you justify any failures to act?

TENTH SUNDAY IN ORDINARY TIME

Jesus' brothers and sisters

[June 8, 1997; omitted 2000 (proceed to first Sunday of Lent, p. 32); June 8, 2003]

First Reading: Genesis 3:9–15

Where are you?

The first man has eaten the forbidden fruit, from the tree of knowledge of good and evil (and everything in between). He has succumbed to the temptation to seek to know everything, to become like God, or at least to be like "a god." The man has sinned. But when God confronts God's most cherished creatures, the man and woman, things get worse. The man blames the woman, and she blames the serpent. The first sin is a pride that is also idolatry, when the person decides "I should be a god." The second sin is an attempt to escape responsibility. Maybe that is a big part of the human condition: We demand to be our own gods, but we also make excuses when things go wrong. Given this sorry state of affairs, it seems a marvel that God has commuted the sentence to hard labor.

Responsorial Psalm: Psalm 130:1–2, 3–4, 5–6, 7–8

Second Reading: 2 Corinthians 4:13–5:1

...our inner being is renewed each day.

Paul cites Psalm 115:1: "I believed, so I spoke." The remaining verses repeat what Paul has learned in hard years of preaching, healing, administering, and in doing theology. He states the essence of his belief, and in so doing he gives shape to Christian doctrine: Our destiny is to be raised up with Jesus, to be in the presence of God. Everything in the created world is ordered for our benefit: Shall we use all things gratefully, for God's glory? We look beyond transitory appearances. When our "earthly tent" is destroyed we enter the dwelling which God has prepared for us. This image reflects Paul's livelihood as tentmaker (Acts 18:3).

Gospel: Mark 3:20–35

...every sin will be forgiven....

Jesus returns home with the disciples, and a crowd so presses upon them that they cannot get anything to eat. His family comes to take charge of him, thinking him out of his mind. Scribes from Jerusalem pronounce him possessed by Beelzebul, empowered by the prince of demons. Thus placed on trial, Jesus defends himself with a question: How can Satan expel Satan? As strife-torn kingdom or divided household must fall, so Satan, if he endures mutiny in his ranks. Jesus' works are so plainly good that they cannot serve the evil one in any way.

Then he turns on the scribes, his most impressive accusers. Every sin will be forgiven, and every blasphemy, but anyone who blasphemes against the Holy Spirit will not be forgiven. Jesus' acts of healing and casting out demons, of compassion and liberation, of giving life, suggest the presence of the Holy Spirit, not of demons. To deny this is to commit a sin far worse than Adam's, for Adam has been given a second chance.

The reading ends on a disturbing note. Jesus' family sends word to him to come out of the house. His response dismisses them, even as it embraces a larger "family": "Anyone who does the will of God is my brother or my sister."

Mark may have included this detail because the primitive church had to deal with the embarrassing fact of Jesus' abandonment by family and neighbors. It intensifies the evangelist's portrait of Jesus as a lonely and misunderstood figure. It also shows Jesus emerging from a difficult situation as the standard by which all the world is to be judged. The evidence is as plain as the good works that Jesus has done. He embodies the Holy Spirit of God, and you must respond to him in some way. To dismiss or accuse him is to turn your back on what is evident, to commit a blasphemy against the Holy Spirit. This sin is unforgivable because it refuses to allow God to do God's work. But to do the will of God is to be embraced as Jesus' brother or sister.

Questions for Reflection

•What sin tempts you most severely? With what kind of sin do you struggle the most often? How do you avoid sin? How do you defend yourself against temptation?

•How readily do you accept responsibility for your actions and choices? What improvements can you make in this regard, if any?

•How do you use the things of God's created world? How well do your choices and actions display gratitude and a desire for God's glory?

•How do you respond to Jesus' action in the world?

ELEVENTH SUNDAY IN ORDINARY TIME

Of seed, branch, and kingdom

[June 15, 1997; omitted 2000; June 15, 2003]

First Reading: Ezekiel 17:22–24

As I, the Lord, have spoken, so will I do.

These verses present the concluding third of a compact and powerfully crafted literary unit. The first third (17:1–11) tells of a great eagle who has stolen the crest from the cedar and set it in a foreign land, and who has planted and nurtured seeds in that land. But these shoots have stretched out toward a different eagle, under whose care they have now produced a majestic vine that is yet doomed by the torrid east wind.

The second section (17:12–21) interprets these figures in specific historical terms, while the third section, today's verses, resumes talk of the crest of the cedar. Caught at the crossroads of empires, Israel will suffer destruction and exile. But after the kings and pharaohs and puppet monarchs have had their way, God will take the topmost shoot from the now-transplanted cedar and plant it on a high mountain. It shall become a majestic cedar, in whose shade every kind of bird will dwell. And then every tree will know that God brings low the high trees and exalts the lowly trees. Even history's eagles must find shade under the branches of God's favored tree.

Responsorial Psalm: Psalm 92:2–3, 13–14, 15–16

Second Reading: 2 Corinthians 5:6–10

We walk by faith, not by sight.

Paul concludes his discussion of the body as a temporary dwelling, a tent. Our life in the body is like living in a tent. The body houses us, but it also inhibits our view. While we dwell in it we are away from the Lord. We do not see, but we walk by faith. Yet we can remain confident of the permanent dwelling that awaits us. Let us always do our best to please God. The text concludes with a reminder of the judgment to come: All of our lives will be revealed before Christ's tribunal. Each person may receive his or her reward, according to the life lived in the temporary dwelling which is the body.

Gospel: Mark 4:26–34
This is how it is with the reign of God.

This kind of episode is rare in Mark's account of the gospel. The other, newer accounts of Matthew, Luke, and John often portray Jesus teaching great crowds at length, and they narrate the substance of that teaching. By contrast, Mark recounts Jesus' widely public teaching mainly in chapter 4, and in smaller bits in chapters 10 and 12. Most of the rest of Mark's account prefers to narrate either Jesus' actions or the teaching he gives privately to the disciples.

Jesus tells a crowd about God's reign with two figures. First, a man scatters seed. He sleeps and rises day after day, and the seed grows without his knowing how. The soil produces, and the man wields his sickle at harvest time. Second, God's reign is like a mustard seed, the smallest of all seeds. When sown, it becomes the largest of shrubs, with room and shade for the birds. The reading concludes with a statement that brackets all of the parables in chapter four: Jesus speaks to the crowds only in parables, in a way they can understand. Meanwhile, he explains things privately to the disciples.

Mark's fourth chapter is dominated by images of seed and growth. We may surmise that Mark intends to portray as the major theme of Jesus' public teaching that the kingdom is already here, and growing. Today's text insists that the kingdom will grow large enough to embrace everyone and everything. Paired with the Ezekiel verses, this text speaks of the inevitability of the kingdom. History will do what it must, and in the end God will accomplish God's own purposes. Those purposes elude our control and understanding, and often they turn our expectations upside down. Finally even the world's eagles must find rest in the shade of God's reign.

Questions for Reflection

•How often has God turned your expectations or understandings upside down? How has this happened?

•How does walking by faith differ from walking by sight? What must you do to walk by faith?

•What image would you use to describe God's reign?

•What does it take to be a citizen in the kingdom of God? What sort of citizen are you? How can you become a better one?

TWELFTH SUNDAY IN ORDINARY TIME

The sea

[June 22, 1997; omitted 2000; June 22, 2003]

First Reading: Job 38:1, 8–11

Who shut within doors the sea...?

His estate and family destroyed, his body covered with sores, Job laments his bad fortune. Some friends hear his complaint, and they offer various reasons to explain his suffering. Job rejects them all, because, as he insists, he is blameless and does not deserve his fate. At last a storm falls upon them, and the Lord speaks out of the storm: "Where were you, Job, when I created the earth? How did it all happen, and who did the measurements?"

The answer, of course, is that the work of creation is so vast that only God could have accomplished it. God's speech continues in today's verses: "Who stopped the rush of the sea when it burst forth from the womb? Who controlled the sea while I swaddled it in darkness and clothed it in clouds? It was I, the Lord, who set limits for the sea, and allowed it to come no further."

Responsorial Psalm: Psalm 107:23–24, 25–26, 28–29, 30–31

Second Reading: 2 Corinthians 5:14–17

The old order has passed away.

Paul states basic convictions: One has died for all, therefore all have died in order to live for the one who was raised up. Anyone who is in Christ is a new creation. The old order has passed away; now all is new.

Gospel: Mark 4:35–41

The Sea of Galilee, which is really a lake, is notorious even today for its sudden and ferocious storms. Channeled and intensified by the steep hills and canyons surrounding the lake, winds can stir up giant waves almost without warning.

The lake plays a dramatic role in Mark's account of the gospel. It is the site where Jesus calls his first disciples (1:16ff., 2:13ff.). It is the platform from which he must teach because crowds press upon him (3:8ff.,

4:1ff.). It swallows up a herd of swine into whom Jesus has cast the demons who have tormented a Gerasene (5:11ff.). The lake is the site of miraculous feedings (6:34ff., 8:1ff.) and the water upon which he walks (6:45ff.). The lakefront city of Capernaum hosts the beginning of Jesus' career (2:21ff.) and many other episodes. And in this text, the lake is a catalyst that reveals Jesus' true identity. Having taught a great crowd in parables, and his disciples with private explanation while seated in a boat, Jesus retreats with the disciples toward the opposite shore. A squall tosses the boat while Jesus sleeps in the stern. Terrified, the disciples awaken him, and he tells the wind and the sea to be still. Then he asks the disciples why they lack faith, and they wonder aloud who this person can be.

In light of today's first reading, there can be only one answer to the disciples' question. But the episode also raises a direct challenge to us, taking the measure of our faith. The one who once calmed a storm on a middle eastern lake also holds power over all the storms that can trouble human lives. None of our daily ups or downs can affect us in any meaningful way, because our destiny is the kingdom that Jesus has announced. But unless we practice the good habits of prayer and listening, we might not embrace what is offered to us. Amid the storms, we must approach him and listen for his voice. Quiet! Be still!

Questions for Reflection

•How often do you feel sorry for yourself or blame someone else for your luck? How do you think God responds to you? How does God's response to Job offer hints?

•How often do you pray? How do you pray? How often do you make a real effort to be quiet and still?

•What terrifies you? What does the story of Jesus calming the storm suggest that you do with your fear or fears?

•Why has Mark concluded his gospel account's most important description of Jesus' teaching with the story of Jesus calming the storm? What does this narrative structure suggest about our ways of hearing Jesus' teaching today?

THIRTEENTH SUNDAY IN ORDINARY TIME

Life and justice

[July 2, 2000; in 1997 and 2003, replaced by the solemnity of SS Peter and Paul, Apostles, see page 152.]

First Reading: Wisdom 1:13–15, 2:23–24

...justice is undying.

The book of Wisdom contains our Bible's most recent writing that predates Jesus. While accepted by Catholics as a biblical book, Wisdom is not included in Jewish or Protestant Bibles. It represents the thinking of some Jewish teachers in Egypt during the fifty years or so before Jesus' birth. Its influence was certainly felt during his lifetime. The book's treatments of immortality clearly influenced the development of early Christian thought.

Today's verses come from the book of Wisdom's examination of justice. Life, wholesomeness, wisdom, discipline, and justice are interconnected, while folly, death, corruption, carelessness, and injustice also belong together. God did not make death. Rather, death entered the world because of the devil's envy. God fashioned all things on purpose, so that they might live. All created things are wholesome, and there is nothing destructive among them. And justice is undying.

Responsorial Psalm: Psalm 30:2, 4, 5–6, 11, 12, 13

Second Reading: 2 Corinthians 8:7, 9, 13–15

...you may also abound in your work of charity.

These excerpts from Paul's delicately crafted challenge to the church at Corinth also challenge us. First, the apostle congratulates the audience for their riches of faith, discourse, and knowledge. Next, he expresses his wish that their work of charity would be as rich. The implicit critique is that they who enjoy all sorts of advantages have been somewhat selfish.

To drive the point home, Paul reminds them of the favor shown by Jesus Christ. There must be equality. Those who are advantaged must share with those who lack. In time all will balance out. The concluding verse cites Exodus 16:18: He who gathered much had no excess and he who gathered little had no lack.

But Paul also speaks directly to us. He chides us for our occasional selfishness and invites us to abound in our work of charity.

Gospel: Mark 5:21–43

Little girl, get up.

Mark's short account of the gospel achieves extraordinary power, in part because of its use of a variety of literary devices. Here we see one such device, in which two stories play together and against one another simultaneously.

Jairus' daughter is ill, and he summons Jesus. *En route* Jesus is delayed by a woman whose hemorrhage has defied all healing efforts for twelve years. She touches Jesus, and her faith heals her, but word arrives from Jairus' house that the daughter has died. Ignoring the news, Jesus proceeds and expels all doubters. Holding the girl's hand, he calls her back to life. Finally, he tells the astonished family to keep quiet about what they have seen, and to feed their daughter.

In light of today's first reading, these stories identify Jesus with the One who desires eternal life and health for all. They also portray him surrounded by people who press their needs upon him. Amid mounting pressures, Jesus always acts on behalf of life, health, and justice. And in the crunch of the crowd, Jesus always recognizes those who seek his help, in faith.

Questions for Reflection

•What evidence tells you that all created things are good? How do you appreciate the divinely given goodness in things as you conduct your day-to-day business? In what ways do you sometimes fail to appreciate the goodness of creation?

•Why are life and justice simply different facets of the same reality?

•What are your real riches? What place do you make for charitable work, among your riches? How can you improve your charitable work?

•What have you asked of Jesus lately? What response have you received, if any? How do you ask?

FOURTEENTH SUNDAY IN ORDINARY TIME

What sort of welcome?

[July 6, 1997; July 9, 2000; July 6, 2003]

First Reading: Ezekiel 2:2–5

They shall know that a prophet has been among them.

The book of Ezekiel begins with a detailed description of a "vision of the likeness of the glory of the Lord" (1:28). The vision is like a man enthroned, surrounded by what seem to be a rainbow and fiery four-headed creatures riding chariots. Falling prostrate, Ezekiel hears a voice that tells him: "Son of man, stand up!"

Today's verses begin with spirit entering Ezekiel and causing him to stand. The voice continues: "I send you to the rebellious Israelites. They are hard and obstinate, but you will tell them what I say. Whether they listen or not, they will know that a prophet has been among them."

Responsorial Psalm: Psalm 123:1–2, 2, 3–4

Second Reading: 2 Corinthians 12:7–10

...in weakness power reaches perfection.

Paul alludes to revelations that he has been privileged to receive, only to insist that he may not boast. As though an instrument of God's will, an angel of Satan has somehow beaten him and kept him from getting proud. In prayer, Paul has asked to be rid of this thorn in the flesh, and the response has been, "My grace is enough for you, for in weakness power reaches perfection." So Paul has become content with weakness, mistreatment, distress, persecutions, and difficulties. He knows that when he is powerless the power of Christ rests upon him.

Gospel: Mark 6:1–6

No prophet is without honor except in his native place.

We can envision Mark's description of Jesus' public ministry by means of two trajectories. The first is acceptance, and the other rejection. In the early chapters, Jesus is a powerful hero, accepted by staggering numbers of people. But even from the beginning, the more powerful and more violent undercurrent of rejection gathers force. This trajectory accelerates to the passion story, which culminates, of course, in Jesus' death on the cross.

The theme of acceptance is evident in the pace of Mark's account. Beginning with his baptism and an extended period in the wilderness, Jesus bursts onto the scene in Galilee. He teaches and heals and announces the kingdom of God. The pace is fast and furious, and it only accelerates. As last Sunday's gospel reading portrayed, Jesus can barely move, for all the people throwing their needs at him. On one level, he enjoys enormous popularity. He is accepted.

Meanwhile, some religious authorities have begun to oppose him, to the extent of summoning experts from Jerusalem to challenge him publicly. More seriously, his family and neighbors have doubted his sanity and tried to apprehend him. And as the passion story reminds us, even his chosen disciples abandon him in the end.

In today's verses a chapter closes in Jesus' life. Returning home, he teaches in the synagogue, where he is rejected. On the one hand, people are amazed. They marvel at his teaching and his miraculous works. On the other hand, these same people reject him, apparently because he is one of them. And he can do nothing there, apart from a few healings, because he is distressed by the lack of faith he finds in his hometown. So he moves on to neighboring villages.

Mark wrote before the formal split between Judaism and the church, but when the divorce was already evident and practically certain to be made formal. This episode probably addresses the embarrassing fact that, while mid-first-century Gentiles converted to the new way in large numbers, a majority of Jesus' own people rejected him. The evangelist has turned an embarrassment into a challenge for the reader. Jesus can work no miracle where he is rejected or where people do not have faith in him. What sort of welcome do we provide?

Questions for Reflection

• How do you think God speaks to you? How often do you hear what seems to be God's direct speech? How often, and in what ways, does God speak more subtly?

• How does your weakness reveal God's power? When did you last choose to allow God to act through your weakness?

• Who are prophets today? Why do you call them prophets? How do you respond to them?

• What sort of welcome do you provide for God? In what ways do you resist or reject God? In what ways are you more receptive?

FIFTEENTH SUNDAY IN ORDINARY TIME

Ministry

[July 13, 1997; July 16, 2000; July 13, 2003]

First Reading: Amos 7:12–15

I was a shepherd and a dresser of sycamores.

The priest Amaziah evicts Amos, insisting that he must never prophesy in Bethel again. For his part, Amos insists that he is no prophet, but that the Lord took him from the flock and told him to prophesy to the Lord's people.

Amos seems to want to disassociate himself from the "prophet-for-hire" corruption that is well-known to Amaziah. Unlike those professional prophets who fall into trances and describe wild visions, Amos does not care what he is called. He insists that genuine prophecy requires neither trance nor vision, nor any of the cultic trappings famous in Bethel. It does require honesty, conviction, and a hard-headed realism with regard to culture, ethics, religion, politics, and economics. For Amos it would make no sense to divide life into segments, as we moderns insist on doing. The prophet speaks what he or she hears from God, and the message always bears cultural, ethical, religious, political, and economic impact.

Responsorial Psalm: Psalm 85:9–10, 11–12, 13–14

Second Reading: Ephesians 1:3–14

In him we were chosen.

This letter, sent in Paul's name, is almost certainly not his work. It exhibits a maturity of thought and language, and reflects historical realities unknown until at least twenty years after the apostle's death. Moreover, the author's use of the word "chosen" differs from Paul's usage. For Paul, the Jews remained the chosen, while this author identifies the church as the new chosen.

Today's verses give us the letter's opening blessing. "Let God be praised. God chose us in Jesus Christ since before the world began, so that we might be blameless and holy. We have been redeemed in Christ. God has given us the wisdom to understand the plan that set Christ as head of all things. We were chosen to be first to hope in Christ. You have been chosen, too, as seen in the fact that you believed when you heard the good news. You were sealed with the Holy Spirit, who is the first installment in a plan by which God will redeem all those who have been chosen."

Gospel: Mark 6:7–13

Jesus...began to send them out two by two.

Mark's account of the gospel portrays Jesus as hero, a figure whose words and wondrous actions attract great throngs of people. But early and spectacular success creates problems. The first one narrated is that it is only with a great deal of difficulty that Jesus can get a moment's rest, or move about from place to place (1:35–37, 1:45). A second problem is resistance (2:6ff.) that culminates in outright rejection (6:1–6, fourteenth Sunday in ordinary time, year B). A third problem is a reflection of the first two: He must proclaim his message on two levels. He speaks to the public in appealing and challenging stories, while explaining those stories to his disciples in greater detail. His message is wonderful, powerful, attractive, but beyond a superficial level it costs a great deal. And a fourth problem is that human need is far too great for Jesus of Nazareth alone to satisfy. He must multiply himself somehow.

This text describes the origin and the essential activities of Christian ministry. Having been tossed out of the synagogue of his childhood, Jesus now concentrates on surrounding villages. He sends the twelve out in pairs, with authority over unclean spirits. He insists that they travel light, and that they stay where they are welcome. When not welcomed, they are to shake the dust from their feet in testimony against the unfriendlies. And the twelve depart to preach repentance, to expel demons, to anoint the sick, and to work cures. Their preaching and activity parallel exactly what Jesus has done up to this point in Mark's account of the gospel, and should be seen as an extension or continuation of Jesus' own mission.

Questions for Reflection

•Who is a prophet today? Whom have you experienced as prophet? Who speaks God's challenging, transforming word to you?

•How do you experience God's favor? For what purpose does God seem to have chosen you?

•How do you participate in and contribute to Christ's ministry? How do you heal? How do you proclaim God's word? What kind of, and how much, baggage do you carry?

SIXTEENTH SUNDAY IN ORDINARY TIME

The shepherd

[July 20, 1997; July 23, 2000; July 20, 2003]

First Reading: Jeremiah 23:1–6

I...will gather the remnant of my flock.

Jeremiah delivers God's warning to the shepherds who mislead and scatter the flock, God's people. They are utterly unlike the shepherd of today's psalm. God will punish these leaders and will gather what remains of the flock to protect them and, borrowing imagery from the first creation story, to allow them to increase and multiply (Genesis 1:22). This prophecy moves in a manner similar to that of the story of the flood (Genesis 6:5–9:28), in which a remnant is saved from amid the wicked of the earth, and a new start is granted. It seems to contradict God's covenant with Noah (Genesis 9:13–17), in which the rainbow is a sign of God's promise not to destroy. This discrepancy is but one of many pieces of evidence suggesting that many different and independent traditions emerged among the ancient Hebrews. Several of these traditions have been gathered into the collection we know as the Bible. Jeremiah does not seem to know the story of the flood.

This text is focused in its last verses, which describe a righteous shoot, a king who will govern wisely, according to justice and mercy. This king will be the instrument of the salvation and security of Judah and Israel. Under his reign Israel and Judah will know God by the name "The Lord of justice."

Responsorial Psalm: Psalm 23:1–3, 3–4, 5, 6

Second Reading: Ephesians 2:13–18

...through him we both have access to the Father.

The author of Ephesians does not struggle with the role of Jewish law in the lives of Christians. Any struggle has long since been resolved. Christ has abolished the law, and in so doing has reconciled all peoples to God, in one body, through the cross that has put to death all differences among peoples. This is clear and forthright doctrine. The good news of peace is announced to all. Everyone enjoys access to God the Father, in the Spirit. The law is irrelevant, as are habits of sovereignty, social class, nationality, and other ways in which people separate themselves from one another. This late-first-century message remains fresh and new and necessary today, as we still indulge in irrelevant habits.

Gospel: Mark 6:30–34

Come...and rest.

Mark frequently places stories within other stories, in order to strengthen both. A good illustration of this literary device occurs in 5:21–43 (thirteenth Sunday in ordinary time), in which the healing of an official's daughter frames and is temporarily interrupted by the story of a woman whose bleeding has not stopped in twelve years. Today's text is the conclusion of another example. Between the commissioning and departure of the twelve (6:7–13, sixteenth Sunday in ordinary time, year B) and their return, Mark has set a most ominous story describing the death of John the Baptizer. The evangelist thus awakens us to the possibility that we who follow Jesus' call to heal and speak in his name may also follow him to martyrdom.

The twelve report to Jesus, and he invites them to come to an out-of-the way place to rest. But as ever in Mark's account, the crush of the crowd makes it impossible for them even to eat. After Jesus and the twelve manage to steal away in a boat, people from all the towns are waiting for them at the supposedly deserted destination. And when he disembarks Jesus sees a vast crowd and he pities them. They are like sheep without a shepherd (Numbers 27:17ff.), and he teaches them many things. Today's first reading has provided a foundation for this encounter. Jesus is the shepherd they seek.

The shepherd who would prefer to retreat with disciples instead chooses to teach. The cost of his and their activities is now abundantly clear. Mark's narrative moves us forward at a breathtaking pace, along with Jesus, toward the cross.

Questions for Reflection

• Why does God seem to prefer to be called "the Lord of justice"? How does this name differ from other names by which we address or speak of God? What does this name say that other names do not say? How does this name challenge us?

• How are people divided from one another? How are nations and whole peoples divided one from another? How do you contribute to or perpetuate divisions among people? How many of the divisions are really necessary?

• What does your discipleship cost you? How do you respond when the cost goes up?

SEVENTEENTH SUNDAY IN ORDINARY TIME

Loaves and fish

[July 27, 1997; July 30, 2000; July 27, 2003]

First Reading: 2 Kings 4:42–44

They shall eat and there shall be some left over.

Elisha the man of God is endowed with a double portion of the power of his mentor, Elijah. With this power he does great things, sustaining a widow through the sale of oil, cleansing a leper, and restoring life to a child who has died. In today's verses he tells a man to distribute barley loaves and grain for the people to eat. The man objects, because there is not enough food. Elisha repeats his order: Give it to the people to eat, for the Lord says that there will be some left over. The food is distributed, all are satisfied, and there is plenty left over.

Responsorial Psalm: Psalm 145:10–11, 15–16, 17–18

Second Reading: Ephesians 4:1–6

There is but one body and one Spirit.

The author may be imprisoned while writing these verses. He (or she?) begs the people of the church of Ephesus to live in ways worthy of their calling. The attributes of worthy living are perfect humility and loving patience. No effort should be spared to preserve the unity of the body of Christ. This unity has been originated by God's own Spirit and binds persons together in peace.

This is a potent social teaching that deepens the letter's declaration on the irrelevance of both law and habits that divide persons and peoples (2:11–22, including the text for the sixteenth Sunday in ordinary time, year B). These verses present a way of evaluating our behavior. The concepts of the Nicene creed, to be proclaimed some two and a half centuries later, are nearly all known to this author. Right behavior is far more important than right words, as this text demonstrates. We exhibit our belief in our actions, much more than in our words.

Gospel: John 6:1–15

Gather up the crusts....

Having read portions of Mark's account of the gospel in a semi-continuous manner for several weeks, here we embark on a different route. In place of Mark's description of Jesus' feeding of five thousand (6:34–44; see also 8:1–10), we read John's version of a miraculous feeding. For the next five weeks, we read from John's chapter 6, which represents the New Testament's most refined eucharistic theology.

The movements of John's account of the feeding parallel exactly those of 2 Kings 4:42–44. Having crossed the Sea of Galilee to Tiberias, Jesus is followed by a crowd. He goes up the mountain with his disciples, and, looking up, he sees the crowd coming toward him. When Jesus asks the disciples to feed the crowd, which numbers five thousand men and their families, they insist that even two hundred days' wages could not buy a mouthful per person. Directing the crowd to recline, Jesus gives thanks and distributes the five loaves and two fish provided by a boy in the crowd. After all have had enough the disciples collect twelve baskets full of pieces. The people begin to call Jesus the promised Prophet, and they wish to make him king. He flees, to be alone.

Although the movements parallel those of the first reading, differences of detail are important. Unlike Elisha, for instance, Jesus does not speak God's word aloud, as though it were something apart from him. He simply does God's word, for that is who he is (John 1:1–18, Christmas Mass during the day). Also, Jesus distributes the bread after giving thanks, as the Greek verb illustrates, by "eucharisting." We should remember that alone among the evangelists, John has not included an "institution of the Eucharist" at the last supper. Instead, an awareness of the Eucharist pervades the entire account. The Eucharist is already the dominant fact of church life by the end of the first century or the beginning of the second, when John writes. Also, Jesus feeds a larger number with fewer loaves than Elisha has done. And he distributes fish, the significance of which continues to be debated.

Questions for Reflection

•How can you help to preserve unity in the many groups with which you associate? What threatens unity? What can you do to maintain your family? What can you do among your associates at work, in volunteer activities, at school? What can you do to preserve unity in the church?

•How often do you give thanks? How has the thanks-giving that is the Eucharist affected your ways of thinking and acting?

•What do you want? What do you ask of God? When has God given you far more than you asked to receive? How has God done this?

EIGHTEENTH SUNDAY IN ORDINARY TIME

Bread of life

[August 3, 1997; Replaced by Transfiguration, 2000 (see page 154); August 3, 2003]

First Reading: Exodus 16:2–4, 12–15

I will...rain down bread from heaven for you.

Every spring, insects feed themselves on tamarisk trees in the Sinai. Their secretions resemble honey. The resulting crusty substance is known as manna, as it has been known since time immemorial.

As Moses leads Israel toward the promised land, the people are hungry, and they know nothing of manna. They complain because they can remember a time in their not very distant past when they were able to eat all they wanted by the stoves in their homes in Egypt. Although they grumble to Moses, really they are complaining against God. But God assures Moses that the people will eat meat in the twilight, and bread in the morning. The seasonal migration of quail arrives from Europe that evening, and the tamarisk drops its manna at dawn. This is the bread that will fill them so that the people may know that the Lord is their God.

However else we might be able to explain it, this manna is a heavenly meal. It is also connected inseparably to a community enacting God's word. It is a miracle for a hungry people, slaves who have escaped their bondage in response to God's call. It is also a test for this people, who will not eat if they fail to follow instructions.

In different words, the manna story displays the fundamentals of what we would later call "sacrament." It describes a community struggling to live faithfully—which can be understood in more than one way—and God's presence is revealed.

Responsorial Psalm: Psalm 78:3–4, 23–24, 25, 54

Second Reading: Ephesians 4:17, 20–24

You must put on a new self created in God's image.

Continuing to teach the church at Ephesus, site of an important temple to Artemis, the author declares that the Christians there cannot live like pagans any longer. These verses set a "fresh, spiritual way of thinking" in opposition to the "empty minds" that characterize pagan life. Verses 18 and 19, omitted from this text, describe the consequences of pagan ignorance. Christians should have learned to set aside the old self of illusion and desire: This is the real work of converting to the Christian way, and immersion in Christ's death and resurrection. The final verse describes what truth accomplishes when it is embodied in the lives of Christians: justice and holiness. This couplet echoes the best of Hebrew prophecy.

The challenge to an ancient Asia Minor church is our challenge as well. There remains much that we must abandon, while we allow Christ to clothe us in new selves. We must think and act in God's image, expressing justice and holiness born of truth.

Gospel: John 6:24–35
I myself am the bread of life.

John portrays these scenes: Jesus feeds a crowd of five thousand families; he sails away to escape the press of the crowd; the crowd chases after him in boats; after what is sure to have been a lengthy search they find him on the other side of the lake.

They ask him three questions, and he answers only indirectly. To the first, "When did you come here?" he tells them that they must work for imperishable food. To the second question, "What must we do to perform God's works?" he replies, "Have faith in the One he sent." And to their third question, "What sign, like manna, will you give us?" Jesus teaches that his Father gives bread from heaven that gives life to the world.

To their request for this bread of life, he teaches that he is that bread. Whoever comes to him shall never be hungry, and whoever believes in him will not thirst.

Questions for Reflection

• When have you complained to God? Why did you complain? What sort of responses have you received?

• What is a sacrament? How does God reveal the divine presence in the world?

• In what ways is our culture a pagan culture? What "empty minded" things command major investments of time and resources? What pagan habits remain active in your life? How can you change things for the better? How can you do justice and holiness?

• How does your belief in Jesus oblige you? What are God's works? Which of God's works are you especially well-suited to do?

NINETEENTH SUNDAY IN ORDINARY TIME

Eternal life

[August 10, 1997; August 13, 2000; August 10, 2003]

First Reading: 1 Kings 19:4–8

Get up and eat.

Although the stories about him are brief (1 Kings 17–21), Elijah is a giant, heroic figure. His every move takes place on an epic stage. He bursts onto the scene to announce to the king that the land will be choked by drought until he commands rain in God's name. It is probable that the king's theft of Naboth's land through political intrigue and murder (recounted at the end of the Elijah stories) is but one of many reasons for the prophet's outrage. By standing up to the king, Elijah earns the wrath of the king's wife, the Phoenician princess Jezebel. After hiding out during the drought, and at one point restoring life to the son of a widow, he proposes a mountaintop contest between himself and the prophets of Jezebel's god, Baal. Their incantations fail utterly, while his altar of the Lord draws lightning and a rainstorm. Having humiliated the prophets of Baal, Elijah directs their executions and runs for his life to escape the evil Jezebel. We find him under a broom tree, one day's journey into the desert, praying for death. After a nap, Elijah feels a messenger's touch and hears a command to eat. He eats the hearth cake provided, drinks water, and falls asleep again. The messenger wakens him, and orders, "Get up and eat, or the journey will be too long for you." Strengthened, he walks forty days and nights to God's mountain, Horeb.

This story calls to mind Israel's epic journey from slavery to freedom, and into covenant with God. The hearth cake reminds us of manna (Exodus 16, eighteenth Sunday in ordinary time, year B), while the prophet's march to Horeb evokes Israel's forty years in the wilderness. Ahab and Jezebel have rendered the ancient covenant almost meaningless, and Elijah fights against them to restore what is proper. In this context, the divinely provided food is an instrument of restoration.

Responsorial Psalm: Psalm 34:2–3, 4–5, 6–7, 8–9

Second Reading: Ephesians 4:30–5:2

Follow the way of love.

The author tells us not to sadden the Holy Spirit with whom we have been sealed. We must replace bitterness, passion and anger, harsh words, slander, and malice with kindness, compassion, and mutual forgiveness. We must imitate God, as God's dear children. Christ has given himself for us.

Gospel: John 6:41–51

I am the bread of life.

The most recent of the four gospels, John's account illustrates the divorce that separates Christians and Jews in the late first century. Jesus is a Galilean Jew, and yet this curious episode speaks of the Jews as distant, as people alien to the gospel's audience, and, worse, as opponents. They murmur because he claims to be the bread of life. Echoing Mark 6:1–6 (fourteenth Sunday in ordinary time, year B) they express their contempt for this hometown boy. Jesus' insistence that no one has ever seen the Father seems to repudiate some aspects of Jewish tradition. Its echoes of the first letter of John (1 John 4:12, seventh Sunday of Easter, year B) also tend to reinforce the traditional judgment that epistle and gospel account are the work of the same author. And in the middle of his discourse on bread, Jesus speaks of "your ancestors," as though he is not one of them. Since this hostile tone continues through the rest of chapter 6, we will encounter it again next week and on the following Sunday.

Even so, there is much of value here. Jesus' discourse presents the New Testament's most developed eucharistic theology. First he insists that faith rests upon grace. Next he establishes a link between belief and eternal life. He repeats his assertion that he is the bread of life (see also John 6:35, eighteenth Sunday in ordinary time, year B). He draws a distinction between the manna of the exodus and the bread of heaven: Anyone who eats this bread will live forever.

Questions for Reflection

•What do you tend to do when you are afraid? How often do you feel sorry for yourself? What gets you moving again? How does God seem to be involved in these events?

•What does the Eucharist give that is utterly new?

•What must you do to accept Jesus' offer of eternal life?

Twentieth Sunday in Ordinary Time

Flesh and blood

[August 17, 1997; August 20, 2000; August 17, 2003]

First Reading: Proverbs 9:1–6

Come, eat of my food.

The collection we know as "proverbs" introduces the notion of Wisdom, portraying her as a lady who visits some persons while avoiding others. Later developments of this portrayal, in our books of Sirach and Wisdom, seem to provide clues leading to the Christian discovery of the Holy Spirit.

Here, Lady Wisdom has built her house and set forth a banquet. She has sent out her maids to invite guests: "Come, eat my food and drink my wine. Give up foolishness, in order to live, and advance in the way of understanding." She invites all, but only some accept her invitation.

Responsorial Psalm: Psalm 34:2–3, 10–11, 12–13, 14–15

Second Reading: Ephesians 5:15–20

Be filled with the Spirit.

During ordinary time, epistle readings rarely coincide with the first reading or gospel, because the lectionary has organized them on a separate calendar. Today's epistle, however, urges Christians to not act like fools. In message if not in imagery, it echoes the first reading.

"Watch how you behave," the writer tells us. "Do not act foolishly, but thoughtfully. We live in evil times, so you must make the most of the opportunities presented to you. Abandon your ignorance and try to discern the will of the Lord. Avoid drunkenness and the misbehavior that comes of it. Be filled with the Spirit. Worship together and give thanks to God always and for everything, in Jesus's name."

Gospel: John 6:51–58

For my flesh is real food and my blood real drink.

Today's first verse repeats the last verse of last Sunday's gospel: "I am the living bread from heaven. If you eat this bread, you will live forever. The bread I give is my flesh, for the life of the world."

Now we see the response: "Jews" quarrel among themselves, wondering how Jesus can possibly give his flesh to eat. On the face of it, Jesus' claim makes no sense. It offends some ears, and even seems intended to offend. Inch by inch, John's sixth chapter drives a wedge between Jew and Christian. At the center of the dispute lies the Eucharist, and all that it signifies.

And Jesus only turns up the heat: "If you do not eat my flesh and drink my blood, you have no life in you. But if you do eat and drink, then I will raise you up on the last day. My flesh is real food, and my blood real drink. This is the bread of heaven. Unlike your ancestors, anyone who eats this food will live forever."

Jesus seems to repudiate all of the Jewish tradition. We must read these words sensitively, however. Written late in the first century or early in the second, and long after the formal separation of church and synagogue, they intend an uncompromised description of Christian belief over against a backdrop that happens to be Jewish. It is probable that this clear statement of eucharistic theology means to refute the various "Gnostic" movements of the time, all of which negate the body. Unfortunately, the statement strikes out at the Jews.

We can and should ask ourselves how we hear these hard words. Do we wish somehow to soften Jesus's graphic choice of words like "flesh" and "blood"? We must not and may not do that. Since the first century, Christians have held without compromise that the Eucharist is Jesus Christ, God become human, and really present in bread and wine. The real dispute in this reading is waged within each person. It is not between Christian and Jew, but between belief and failure to believe.

Questions for Reflection

•How do you respond to Wisdom's dinner invitation?

•How do you try to discern the will of the Lord? What helps you? Who guides you? How can you tell whether you hear God's will?

•What aspect of Catholic belief is most difficult for you? If it is not the Eucharist, what other things do you find difficult? How do you resolve your difficulties?

•How does your participation in Christ's meal oblige you? What must you do, because you eat and drink?

Twenty-First Sunday
in Ordinary Time

God's holy one

[August 24, 1997; August 27, 2000; August 24, 2003]

First Reading: Joshua 24:1–2, 15–17, 18

...we also will serve the Lord,...who is our God.

These excerpts portray the climax of the book of Joshua. Having followed Moses to the promised land, now under Joshua's leadership, the people of Israel have occupied the land. They have driven out indigenous peoples, and they control a fertile and strategically important territory.

Joshua's climactic speech at Shechem summarizes the history of the people to that point. It interprets the lives of the patriarchs, the exodus, and the conquest of Palestine as powerful proof of God's action on behalf of the people. Joshua poses a choice: "Decide today whether you will serve the Lord or the pagan gods of either your distant ancestors or the peoples whom you have conquered." The response is unhesitant and powerful: "The Lord has done great things for us, leading us out of slavery and into our new home. We will serve the Lord as our parents and grandparents have done, for the Lord is our God."

Responsorial Psalm: Psalm 34:2–3, 16–17, 18–19, 20–21, 22–23

Second Reading: Ephesians 5:21–32

Defer to one another out of reverence for Christ.

The author invites the audience to think of the family as a hierarchical society. The husband is portrayed as head, just as Christ is head of the church. Wives are to be submissive. Today, many people object to these ideas, and rightly so. Too often "submission" is a form of servitude. Men and women are supposed to be equal, they reason. As a result, some biblical verses seem to pose serious obstacles to belief.

The text's first verse may help. It directs Christians to defer to one another out of reverence for Christ. Some translations even insist that we submit to one another, communicating a network of relationships that is quite different from hierarchy. The family is supported on a foundation of mutuality, exactly the kind of sharing or equality that we moderns say we desire. Equality is not a modern development, however. It is an ancient principle made possible because God is the head of all. We can hear it in today's epistle, if we do not allow a few of its words to distract us.

Gospel: John 6:60–69

...we are convinced that you are God's holy one.

The final scene in John's sixth chapter portrays murmuring, not by "Jews," but by some of Jesus' disciples. They wonder how anyone can take seriously this talk about eating his flesh and blood. They illustrate that it is a struggle for anyone, even for Jesus' most intimate associates, to deal with Christian teaching concerning the Eucharist. As always, Jesus intensifies the struggle. "On top of everything I have taught you about my flesh and my blood and eternal life," he says, "what would you do if you saw me ascend to to where I was before? The spirit gives life, while the flesh is useless. My words are spirit and life."

This teaching is just too much for some. Jesus' talk of ascension and enlivening spirit make plain that he is not only a divine emissary. He is, as Peter says, God's holy one. This is the essence of Christian faith. But many disciples break away, never to return. Jesus poses to the Twelve a choice similar to that described in the first reading. Simon Peter responds, referring to Jesus in the same way that the Jewish tradition has always spoken of God: "You have the words of eternal life. You are God's holy one."

While this climactic response concludes today's reading, the chapter offers two more verses, describing the intent of Judas Iscariot. We face a fundamental choice in uncompromised terms: We may believe and live, or we may choose another path.

Questions for Reflection

•What great things has the Lord done for you? What other things has the Lord done in history, that are good for the world and for you?

•How well do you defer to others? Especially, how hard do you try to defer to persons in your family? What improvements can you make?

•What aspects of our faith cause you to murmur in discomfort, or even disbelief? How do you deal with these things?

Twenty-Second Sunday in Ordinary Time

The law

[August 31, 1997; September 3, 2000; August 31, 2003]

First Reading: Deuteronomy 4:1–2, 6–8

Observe them carefully....

Poised at the entrance to the promised land, Moses begins the first of his long addresses to the people of Israel. Today's verses are extracted from a long, dramatic prologue to the commandments of the Lord. The statutes and decrees are given so that the people may live and take possession of the land given to them. The people must not alter in any way what is commanded. Careful observance of God's law will prove to all the nations that Israel is a great, wise, and intelligent people. For no god is as close to the people as the Lord is to Israel, and no law is as just as the Lord's law.

The scene reminds us of last week's first reading, in which Joshua addresses Israel after the conquest. Actually that episode portrays a renewal of the entire covenantal drama enacted in Deuteronomy, which is initiated here. In effect, one week later, we step backward in history to witness the most solemn circumstances in which the law has been proposed.

Responsorial Psalm: Psalm 15:2–3, 3–4, 4–5

Second Reading: James 1:17–18, 21–22, 27

Act on this word.

James' brief letter is unusual. Unlike other epistles, it only rarely mentions Jesus by name. Some scholars have suggested that it is really a Jewish tract, "baptized" as it were with a few Christian references. Most do not accept this suggestion, however. The letter's language is extremely fine, obviously the work of a well-educated writer. Even so, it carries few extended thoughts, instead presenting a jumble of exhortations. It is a powerful moral tract that argues repeatedly on behalf of faithful action. More forcefully than any other New Testament book, the letter of James echoes the classic Hebrew prophets, insisting that faith must be made visible in action.

Today's verses insist that every worthwhile gift comes from above. The Father of the heavenly luminaries brings us to birth with a word, so that we may be the firstfruits of his creation. We must welcome the word that has taken root in us. And we must act on this word, or we deceive ourselves. Echoing the prophet Amos' restless pursuit of justice, the author tells us that pure worship consists in caring for orphans and widows and keeping ourselves unspotted before our God and Father.

Gospel: Mark 7:1–8, 14–15, 21–23
Hear me, all of you, and try to understand.

After reading John's account for several weeks, we return to Mark's account of the gospel with excerpts from chapter seven. Having fed five thousand families, Jesus has walked on the surface of the Sea of Galilee and healed many at Gennesaret. Now he is confronted by some Pharisees and scribes. They ask Jesus why his disciples eat without obeying purity laws, and he responds angrily: "You are hypocrites! Isaiah spoke of you, people who honor God with your lips, but your hearts are distant [see Isaiah 29:13]. You disregard God's commandment but cling to human tradition."

Then he addresses the crowd: "Nothing outside can defile you, but what you produce inside you can mark you as impure." With this bold statement, Jesus seems to have dismissed whole portions of the Mosaic law. He certainly seems to contradict the statement in today's first reading that the people must observe the laws carefully. But he is really interpreting the law in a manner similar to the great Hebrew prophets, who insisted that the true test of faith is righteous action. In the end Jesus responds to a request from the disciples, explaining his interpretation of the law: "Consider all the evil things people can do. These are the things that defile."

Questions for Reflection

• If law and precepts are given solemnly, how can anyone ever presume to alter them? Why would anyone try to interpret the law of Moses? Why would any Catholic today dare to dissent from any of the church's teaching?

• With regard to Jesus' word, what must you do to avoid deceiving yourself?

• What right does Jesus have to dismiss parts of the law? Why does he do this, right after calling others hypocrites for their uses of the law?

• How do you live your faith?

Twenty-Third Sunday in Ordinary Time

Be opened!

[September 7, 1997; September 10, 2000; September 7, 2003]

First Reading: Isaiah 35:4–7

Here is your God.

Although prophecy often speaks in the future tense, it is usually not a prediction. The prophet speaks the word of God to the whole gamut of circumstances. The word analyzes cultural, ethical, economic, and political issues as well as religious ones, because to the prophet, all these dimensions of life are bound up together. The word also challenges the people to avoid a wrong course and to take action that God prefers. Thus when the people of Israel have forgotten their purpose, the prophet warns them of God's anger. When the people have suffered, the prophet offers God's consolation.

Today's verses follow Isaiah's piercing analyses of the political fortunes of the neighboring nations. God will erase them all, and indeed God's own people will be purged. But those who are frightened must hear: "Be strong! Do not fear! Your God comes to save you. When God comes, the blind will see, the deaf will hear, the lame will dance, the mute will speak, and the desert will bloom."

Responsorial Psalm: Psalm 146:7, 8–9, 9–10

Second Reading: James 2:1–5

...your faith...must not allow of favoritism.

The epistle of James presents a consistent and passionate appeal for justice. Here the author poses a situation: Suppose two people appear among us, one dressed well, and the other in shabby clothes. If we play favorites, we discriminate. We act like judges who hand down corrupt decisions. The reading concludes by reminding us that God chose the poor to be rich in faith and heirs of the kingdom.

The point runs deeper than our taste in fashion. Our faith is made visible by our actions, far more than by our words. Our faith does not permit us to play favorites in any way, because only God can judge justly. If our faith is to be worth anything at all, we must act justly. We know how to do that, because since the beginning of time God has called us to assist and to honor the widowed, the orphaned, the poor, and all who are afflicted in the world.

Gospel: Mark 7:31–37
Be opened!

Mark's account of the gospel draws its tone from the ending of the first chapter. At the beginning of his career, Jesus has cured a leper and ordered him not to say anything about it. But the man cannot contain himself, and Jesus's fame has spread like wildfire. From this point on he cannot enter any town openly, and he must go to great lengths to find a moment's rest.

Today we see Jesus returning to Galilee from Gentile territory. A deaf and speech-impaired man is brought to him. Probing the ears, spitting, and touching the man's tongue, Jesus groans toward heaven and commands the man's ears to be opened. At once the man's impediments are removed, and the crowd is astonished. Despite all of Jesus's pleas, observers announce the events: He has made the deaf hear and the mute speak.

Any Jewish audience would recognize the importance of this episode. Today's first reading acquaints us with Isaiah's widely known description of God's saving action. People are beginning to see that Jesus is more than a wonder-worker and teacher. He even seems to fulfill hopes cherished for generations.

Questions for Reflection

•In addition to the images described in today's first reading, what signs illustrate God's saving action in the world? What signs suggest that God has acted and continues to act in your life?

•How do you make your faith visible? Which do you do more: Do you talk your faith, or do you act your faith? What would James say to you?

•If you could stand by the sea of Galilee with Jesus, what part of you would he touch, with the words "Be opened"? What things tend to impede you from living the gospel?

TWENTY-FOURTH SUNDAY IN ORDINARY TIME

Servanthood

[September 17, 2000;
Replaced by Triumph of the Cross in 1997 and 2003 (see page 158)]

First Reading: Isaiah 50:4–9

The Lord God is my help.

These verses are nearly the same as the reading used each year on Passion Sunday. They are taken from the third of what are called the "servant songs" in the book of Isaiah. They speak of extreme suffering endured as faithful service: "I gave my back to those who beat me, my cheeks to those who plucked my beard, my face to slaps and spitting. But the Lord is my help, and I am not disgraced. Anyone who opposes me also opposes the One who stands beside me."

From its origins, the church has seen Jesus as the most faithful of servants. He embodies perfectly the poet's words.

Responsorial Psalm: Psalm 116:1–2, 3–4, 5–6, 8–9

Second Reading: James 2:14–18

…the faith that does nothing in practice…is thoroughly lifeless.

Here is the foundation of James' entire letter, presented in rhetorical questions. What good is it to profess faith without practicing it? Such a faith cannot save, can it? What good is it if you greet people who have great needs but do nothing to assist them in their need?

Talk like this could sound "Pelagian," after the early heresy in which persons insisted that they could earn their way to eternal life. Recognizing the danger, the author acknowledges Paul's strong teaching against salvation by works (Romans 4:5–6), and offers a clarification. There can be no opposition between faith and works. The final verse of this reading introduces an argument based on Hebrew tradition. In this argument, which runs to verse 26, James applies the name "ignoramus" to anyone who thinks faith can exist apart from work on behalf of justice. The argument concludes with a parallel: The body without a spirit is dead, and faith without works is dead.

Gospel: Mark 8:27–35

...who do you say that I am?

At Caesarea Philippi, Jesus asks the disciples who they think he is, and Peter responds that Jesus is Messiah. After ordering them not to tell this to anyone, he gives them a new, explicit teaching. Like the servant portrayed in today's first reading, Jesus must suffer. He must be rejected by all the leaders of his time, and he must be executed. He will rise three days later. Peter protests, and Jesus explodes at him: "Get out of my sight, you satan!" These are the strongest words that Jesus uses against anyone, in any of the four accounts of the gospel. It is notable that Mark does not include a detail that Matthew does mention (16:17–20, twenty-second Sunday in ordinary time, year A), as Jesus names Peter the rock upon which the church is to be built. In Mark's account, no one is to be congratulated. Jesus' example remains ever challenging and difficult.

The episode concludes when Jesus summons the crowd and teaches them the basis of discipleship: "To come after me, you must deny yourself and take up your cross. If you lose your life for my sake and for the sake of the gospel, you will save your life."

Together with the transfiguration, this event occupies the midpoint of Mark's account of the gospel. They define the plot for the remainder of the narrative, but they also encapsulize the whole gospel. Our faith requires much more than a confession that Jesus is Messiah. If that is all we can do, then Jesus has very strong words for us. He has not spared even Peter. We must also follow in his footsteps, entering into both his suffering and his glory. And if we who have been privileged refuse to follow him, others will follow in our place.

Questions for Reflection

• When does suffering become virtuous and faithful? When is it something else and something less?

• What is faithful servanthood?

• How good are you at living your faith in your actions? How can you improve?

• Who do you say that Jesus is? What do you do about the faith you profess?

TWENTY-FIFTH SUNDAY IN ORDINARY TIME

Wisdom and foolishness

[September 21, 1997; September 24, 2000; September 21, 2003]

First Reading: Wisdom 2:17–20

...he will defend him....

In medieval times, a woman suspected of witchery was strapped to a chair and held under water for a long time. If she drowned, she was thought to be virtuous, and was mourned. If she survived, however, she was executed promptly, because it was supposed that only a witch could survive inhuman lengths of time under water.

Today's first reading portrays the same kind of cynicism. Confronted by an unnamed just one, the wicked choose to test God. Let us revile and torture the just one, they say, for according to his own words, God will take care of him. Let us put him to a shameful death, in order to find proof of his gentleness and try his patience.

The Bible's newest pre-Christian book thus portrays foolishness in great detail, in order to invite us to embrace its opposite. Wisdom is not judgmental, cynical, or belligerent. Wisdom is a gift of God, faithful and gentle and patient.

Responsorial Psalm: Psalm 54:3–4, 5, 6–8

Second Reading: James 3:16–4:3

...justice is sown in peace for those who cultivate peace.

These verses also contrast wisdom and its opposite. Jealousy and strife accompany inconstancy and all kinds of vileness. Wisdom is innocent, peaceable, lenient, docile, sympathetic, kind, impartial, and sincere. Inviting us to think metaphorically, the author speaks of a harvest: If we cultivate peace, we harvest justice.

Having made the point, James drives it home with a social and political analysis. If we let our inner cravings determine our actions, then we fall into conflict. We even indulge our passions in war. We cannot get what we want, so we resort to violence and murder. But we do not obtain because we do not ask. When we do ask we impose demands, thinking only of our pleasure.

Gospel: Mark 9:30–37

Whoever welcomes a child...welcomes me.

Again Jesus predicts his death and resurrection, and the disciples fail to understand. Perhaps intimidated by the exchange between Peter and Jesus portrayed in last week's gospel, the disciples ask him no further questions. But after witnessing Jesus' transfiguration and his healing of a boy with a demon, they argue among themselves about their own importance. The narrative asks us to envision Jesus walking along and listening, and not at all liking what he hears.

At Capernaum, he challenges them on their conversation, and they remain silent. He teaches the Twelve that anyone who wishes to rank first must become the servant of all. Then he embraces a child, as if to illustrate: "Whoever welcomes a child welcomes me, and whoever welcomes me welcomes the one who sent me."

Jesus is the personification of Wisdom. Fully aware of the suffering that awaits him, he has already insisted that disciples follow in his footsteps. Over against his example and his teaching, the disciples look like foolishness personified. Now he embraces someone who is helpless, who has no legal standing. And he insists that disciples do the same. To do so is to choose wisdom.

Questions for Reflection

• What aspects of popular opinion are really foolishness? What must you do to act wisely in response to this foolishness?

• What do you cultivate? If not peace and justice, what do you cultivate by your actions?

• Why does peacemaking yield justice? How do you try to get what you want? How do you enact peace and justice in your day-to-day life?

• How often are you tempted to claim greatness for yourself? How do you deal with this temptation?

• How do you follow in Jesus' footsteps? In what ways do you resist following him?

• Whom do you embrace? Who is helpless, defenseless, voiceless? Whom must you embrace? How will you do it?

TWENTY-SIXTH SUNDAY IN ORDINARY TIME

In Jesus' name

[September 28, 1997; October 1, 2000; September 28, 2003]

First Reading: Numbers 11:25–29

Would that all the people of the Lord were prophets.

The book of Numbers narrates Israel's journey from Mt. Sinai to the threshold of the promised land. Israel is a privileged people on the move, who complain almost constantly about their lot. In the eleventh chapter, the people have grown tired of manna and want meat. Moses has grown equally weary of this people and tells God that the burden of carrying them is too great. God's response overwhelms, in every respect. First, God directs Moses to tell the people to sanctify themselves for the meat they will receive, and to assemble seventy elders. Next, God takes some of the spirit from Moses and dispenses it to the elders. Finally, God drives a huge flock of quail in from the sea (see also Exodus 16:2–15, eighteenth Sunday in ordinary time, year B). The greediest people gorge themselves and die.

Today's verses describe the distribution of the spirit. As the spirit comes on the seventy, they prophesy. Chaos results, and Moses has gotten more than he had wanted. But unlike many, he learns. When two men other than the seventy are seen carrying on in what looks like prophetic ecstasy, Joshua urges Moses to stop them. Moses refuses, for he understands that he cannot control the spirit of God. Instead, he wishes that all the people were prophets. It would be good if God bestowed the divine spirit on all the people.

Responsorial Psalm: Psalm 19:8, 10, 12–13, 14

Second Reading: James 5:1–6

See what you have stored up for yourselves.

These verses echo the prophets' blistering critiques of the wealthy, especially those of Amos (see 8:4–8, for example). The wealthy are urged to begin weeping now for the miseries they will face. All your treasures have decayed in their storehouses, says James, and their decay describes what is really in store for you. The wages you withheld from others testify against you, and God has heard. Your luxurious life has fattened you for the day of slaughter. Although there is no clear evidence that James has influenced any of the evangelists, the parable of the rich man and Lazarus (Luke 16:20–31, twenty-sixth Sunday in ordinary time, year C) seems to make the same point in narrative form.

Is this hard message intended for us? If we have pursued our own advantages ahead of peace and justice, then we must take it to heart.

Gospel: Mark 9:38–43, 45, 47–48
Anyone who is not against us is with us.

The issues in this text are the same as those in the first reading. A disciple informs Jesus that a man not of their company has been seen expelling demons in Jesus' name, and that the disciples have tried to stop him. Do not stop him, says Jesus. Anyone who is not against us is with us. Like Moses, Jesus teaches others that God acts in many ways that are beyond the understanding or control of people who are explicitly believers in God.

But this tolerant tone sours quickly. Anyone who preaches and heals in Jesus' name also faces a daunting responsibility. We may not lead others astray. The disciple who misleads others is best off drowned with a millstone. In graphic imagery, Jesus invites the disciples to amputate body parts that cause problems. Clearly, many who do not claim to be disciples can and do teach and heal, as Jesus has done. But we who call ourselves disciples must either set impeccable examples or face dire consequences.

Questions for Reflection

• What have you sought from God? When has God's response overwhelmed you? How has God overwhelmed you?

• What is your attitude toward your riches? Even if you do not consider yourself a wealthy person, you do live in a wealthy society. How much of what you take for granted in your life really also belongs to someone else?

• Who seems to work alongside Jesus, without claiming to be a disciple? Which famous people fit this description? Whom do you know who works alongside Jesus without claiming to be a disciple?

• What are your most important responsibilities as a disciple?

TWENTY-SEVENTH SUNDAY IN ORDINARY TIME

Accept the kingdom

[October 5, 1997; October 8, 2000; October 5, 2003]

First Reading: Genesis 2:18–24

I will make a suitable partner.

In the second creation story (Genesis 2:4b–25) God shapes the man out of clay and places him in a garden, to tend it. The man may eat from all the trees but one. In today's verses God considers a partner for the man, and presents him with various birds and beasts. But none is a suitable partner. Putting the man to sleep, God fashions a rib from the man into a woman. And the man rejoices at having found his partner.

Too much has been made of the story's apparent reversal of nature. Some observers see a distortion of reality in the fact that here the woman is born from the man's body. They cite the story as an example of Hebrew (and Christian) tradition's unfair and unjust bias toward the male. While they may raise a legitimate issue, the real point of the story is partnership. An old rabbinic interpretation of the story insists that the rib is a powerful symbol of equality. If God had chosen to fashion the woman from the man's head, says this analysis, or his hand or his foot, the two humans would not be equal. One partner would either dominate the other, as head, or serve the other as hand or foot. But the rib symbolizes the heartbeat that man and the woman share. Moreover, the Hebrew word describing the man's partner is best understood as "beside and opposite." We are not supposed to be alone. We need one another, and no gender is superior.

Responsorial Psalm: Psalm 128:1–2, 3, 4–5, 6

Second Reading: Hebrews 2:9–11

...he is not ashamed to call them brothers.

Citing Psalm 8, the anonymous author of the letter to the Hebrews reminds us that Jesus was made one of us, a little lower than the angels. It was God's will that he die for all our sakes, that he be made perfect through suffering. The one who consecrates, and we who are consecrated, have the same Father. Therefore, Jesus calls us brothers and sisters.

Gospel: Mark 10:2–16

Let the children come to me.

In the first part of this text, Pharisees question Jesus regarding the legality of divorce. The law permits it (Deuteronomy 24:1–4), but Jesus is known to disapprove. It is probable that the Pharisees seek to catch him contradicting the law. It is also possible that they want to trap him into publicly challenging the frequent divorces of the Herod dynasty. In either case, Jesus does seem to give them what they want. He responds that the law accommodates the stubbornness of the Pharisees. Knowing that they are experts in the law of Moses, he also appeals to what the Bible represents as the natural order of creation, citing the story contained in today's first reading. God has placed the man and the woman together. No one should ever dare to part them. In private, he intensifies this message for the disciples: Divorce is tantamount to adultery.

These are radical, uncompromising words. Other New Testament sources suggest exceptions (Matthew 5:32 and 19:9; 1 Corinthians 7:10–16), but the basic premise remains intact. We ought not to break what God has joined.

The second part of this text portrays Jesus welcoming children. When the disciples scold, Jesus grows indignant, because, as usual, they have failed to understand him and his message. The kingdom belongs to children and to those who accept the kingdom as children would do. And how is that? In the time of Jesus, as today, children are powerless, voiceless, defenseless, utterly dependent, and receptive. Even so, they are persons possessed of the dignity given to all human persons. Children are partners with their elders, deserving citizens of the kingdom. To accept our places in the kingdom, it seems that we too must allow ourselves to be dependent and receptive. *Children can teach us a lesson*

Questions for Reflection

• When is it good for you to be alone? When do you want companionship?

• How do people become partners? How does partnership differ from other patterns of relationship?

• How do you respond to Jesus's words about divorce?

• What will you have to do to become like a child?

TWENTY-EIGHTH SUNDAY IN ORDINARY TIME

God's word

[October 12, 1997; October 15, 2000; October 12, 2003]

First Reading: Wisdom 7:7–11

...the spirit of Wisdom came to me.

The book of Wisdom is sometimes ascribed to King Solomon. Since this book was composed during the first century before Jesus, however, it cannot be Solomon's work. It was written eight centuries after Solomon's death, in Greek, the language of daily life through most of the Roman empire. In vocabulary, style, and content it resembles other works of Hellenistic Judaism, particularly those produced in Alexandria, the great center of learning on the Nile delta.

These verses illustrate a practice common to many books in our Bible: An author uses the name of a revered historical figure, both to honor that figure and to claim authority for the newer work. These verses teach by interpreting Solomon's widely respected gift of wisdom (see 1 Kings 3:3–9) in a way that serves a radically changed social context. "I prayed for wisdom," says the king, "preferring her over any of the treasures available to me. Yet Wisdom has brought me unimaginable riches." Here Wisdom is much more than an ancient king's legendary prudence and judgment. Wisdom is nothing less than a proper relationship with God, available to everyone. Look at what Wisdom did for Solomon, says the author. Imagine what Wisdom can do for you!

Responsorial Psalm: Psalm 90:12–13, 14–15, 16–17

Second Reading: Hebrews 4:12–13

God's word is living and effective.

In one of the most powerful images in the New Testament, God's word is compared to a two-edged sword. It pierces and divides soul and spirit, joint and marrow, and judges the heart's contents. Nothing is hidden from God, to whom we are accountable.

We cannot be sure that the author knows John 1:1ff. (Christmas Mass during the day), in which the Word is eternal with God and identical with God. It is certain, however, that the author knows and depends upon images familiar to any Jewish audience. God's word accomplishes the purpose for which it has been sent (Isaiah 55:10–11, Easter Vigil and fifteenth Sunday in ordinary time, year A). God's word is a matter of life or death (Deuteronomy 32:46–47). God's mouthpiece the prophet is a sword (Isaiah 49:2), and God's wisdom is a warrior bearing a sword (Wisdom 18:15–16).

Clearly, God's word is bigger than any book, than any collection of books, bigger than all the words ever spoken or written. God's word lives and makes things happen. God's word penetrates the very fiber of our being. It is the standard by which we are measured.

Gospel: Mark 10:17–30
There is one more thing you must do.

Just as the first reading interprets and expands an ancient Hebrew text, we use this text from Mark to interpret and expand the first reading. A man asks Jesus what he must do to share in eternal life. He recites some of the commandments, and the man replies that he has kept them faithfully. You must do one more thing, says Jesus. Sell your possessions, give the money to the poor, and come and follow me. The wealthy man walks away, dejected.

Jesus stuns the disciples with the teaching that follows. It is easier for a camel to pass through the eye of a needle than for a wealthy person to enter God's kingdom. Still, with God all things are possible. Finally, Peter observes that, unlike the rich man, the disciples have put aside everything to follow Jesus. Jesus' reply suggests that he sees through the emptiness of Peter's promises: Whoever really does follow him will receive boundless rewards in this age, as well as everlasting life. Wisdom consists in doing "one more thing," giving up everything to follow Jesus.

Questions for Reflection
• What do you desire, more than anything else?
• When God looks at you, whom and what does God see? When God's word slips into your innermost secrets, how do you measure up?
• What are you doing right now, to gain eternal life?
• What one thing more must you do? What will it cost you to do this?

TWENTY-NINTH SUNDAY IN ORDINARY TIME

True greatness

[October 19, 1997; October 22, 2000; October 19 2003]

First Reading: Isaiah 53:10–11

...the will of the Lord shall be accomplished through him.

These verses are also part of the conclusion of Good Friday's first reading. They come from the final "servant song" created by an unknown poet and inserted into the book of Isaiah. The song describes and interprets suffering endured by one person for the sake of others.

This text's first verse suggests that God causes suffering, but the Christian refutes any such suggestion. The remaining verses portray a paradox: The one who gives his life as an offering for sin shall live long and fulfill God's will. The servant shall see light because of his affliction, and his suffering will justify many.

Responsorial Psalm: Psalm 33:4–5, 18–19, 20, 22

Second Reading: Hebrews 4:14–16

...let us hold fast to our profession of faith.

The letter to the Hebrews makes no claim to be Paul's work. By virtue of its vocabulary and its particular address to Jewish Christians, it has always been considered the work of someone other than Paul, who is known to have labored mightily to evangelize the Gentiles. It is written in perhaps the most fluent prose of all New Testament books. It is also the New Testament's most obviously supersessionist work, teaching that Jewish tradition has been superseded, that is, has been made obsolete, and has been replaced, by Christian revelation. Many passages seem to modern eyes quite anti-Jewish.

Christ's priesthood and sacrifice constitute the main theme of this letter, occupying chapters 3–10. This text captures the gist of the letter's argument. Christ is altogether superior to the priests of the past. Unlike the high priests who have isolated themselves from the weaknesses and temptations of ordinary folks, Jesus has faced everything we face. He is the great high priest who has passed through the heavens. Let us therefore approach the divine throne in confidence. He who has become one of us offers mercy, favor, and help.

Gospel: Mark 10:35–45

Can you drink the cup I shall drink...?

After a very difficult teaching about riches (10:17–30, twenty-eighth Sunday in ordinary time, year B) Jesus tells the twelve again about his passion. Without skipping a beat, James and John pose a question that is the focus of today's reading: "When you enter your glory, may we sit on either side of you?" Sometimes indignant over requests like this, here Jesus is more gentle. He asks: "Can you drink from my cup, can you be baptized in the same pain as I?" They insist that they can, and he affirms their self-confidence. But he adds that he cannot give what they ask.

Meanwhile the other disciples grow angry with James and John. Jesus calls them all together and talks about authority. The Gentiles are accustomed to leaders who throw their weight around, but disciples must be different. If you want to be great, you must serve all the rest. With the disciples, we learn here a little bit more about what we must do to follow Jesus. We cannot seek personal gain of any kind, despite Jesus' magnificent promises. We must act with a pure and simple motive. We must serve, perhaps even in the manner of the legendary servant described in the first reading. We may even have to give our lives for others.

Questions for Reflection

•What purpose directs your life? How is your purpose made evident in the ways in which you earn and spend money? What purpose is revealed in the ways in which you relate to people? How do you spend leisure time, and what does this way of acting tell about your purpose?

•When you pray, how do you approach Jesus? What sort of high priest does Jesus seem to be?

•What authority do you bear? How did you gain this authority? What do you do with it? Whom do you serve? How do you serve? What can you do to serve God and humanity more effectively and more genuinely?

THIRTIETH SUNDAY IN ORDINARY TIME

A blind beggar

[October 26, 1997; October 29, 2000; October 26, 2003]

First Reading: Jeremiah 31:7–9

Behold, I will bring them back.

Conquered and deported, many of the people of Judah have been exiled to Babylon and other far-off places. Jeremiah has remained faithful to his task, warning kings and people alike against insecure alliances and, more gravely, against faithlessness. But his warnings have been ignored. First, Babylon's defeat of the Egyptian army has made Judah's alliance with Egypt look foolhardy. Second, the vassal kings installed in Judah by Babylon have permitted the cults of various idols to dominate. Third, these same vassal kings' continued overtures toward Egypt have led to their downfall and to the deportation of large numbers of the people of Judah. But Jerusalem has not yet fallen. Still in the city, Jeremiah offers to the exiles God's promise of a new exodus. Shout for joy, says the prophet, for God will deliver God's people, the remnant of Israel. God will bring them back, from all the places into which they have been scattered. They left in tears. God, their father, will bring them to refreshing water, along a smooth road.

Responsorial Psalm: Psalm 126:1–2, 2–3, 4–5, 6

Second Reading: Hebrews 5:1–6

You are my son.

Immediately following last week's first reading, these verses continue the theme of Jesus as high priest. The high priest represents the people, making sacrifices for the sins of the people, but also for himself. The priest does not appoint himself, but, like Aaron and Melchizedek, he is called by God. Christ did not appoint himself. God called him long ago, in words familiar to every Jew: "You are my son" (Psalm 2:7). "You are a priest forever" (Psalm 110:4).

Gospel: Mark 10:46–52

Your faith has healed you.

A blind beggar sits by a road in Jericho. Learning that Jesus is passing by amid disciples and a large crowd, Bartimaeus calls out. People try to shut him up, but he shouts louder: "Son of David, have pity on me." Jesus stops and directs the disciples to call the beggar to him. They assure Bartimaeus that he has nothing to fear, that he should go to Jesus. He complies, leaving his cloak behind, and he asks for sight. Jesus then tells him to go on his way, since his faith has healed him. And Bartimaeus sees, and follows Jesus.

This episode closes a chapter in Jesus' career. The rest of Mark's account is set in Jerusalem. Up to this point, Jesus has taught and worked miracles, and spoken of the suffering he must endure. From now on, his similar actions anger authorities who conspire against him and kill him. Until now, Jesus has invited others to drop everything and follow him. From now on, the high cost of discipleship becomes clear.

The story of Bartimaeus is pivotal and multi-layered. At face value, it illuminates a beggar's faith, which contrasts with that of the disciples. While they have constantly imposed conditions and demands, the beggar abandons his former way of life without hesitation. It is only in spite of themselves that here the disciples invite the beggar into the encounter that saves him. At another, deeper level, the story sketches the movements that shape the life of any person who would believe in Jesus Christ.

Beginning in utter darkness and having no other choices, we call out to him. Thousands of voices discourage us, and although we may find this fact hard to understand, sometimes those voices belong to the church. We face a critical choice. We may fall silent, or we may persist, as Bartimaeus has done. Jesus always calls us to himself. Sometimes we who are the church do our job and reassure people of this truth, even though they remain in the dark. We abandon our cloaks and all the other desperate or false securities to which we have clung, and we stand before Jesus. At this deep encounter he asks us what we want, and by now we have learned to ask only for what matters most. And the gift is granted without hesitation. Able to see at last, we follow him.

Questions for Reflection

•How often do you call upon Jesus? What or who discourages you from calling him?

•What symbolizes and reinforces your way of life, as the beggar's cloak does for Bartimaeus?

•What does it cost you to follow Jesus? What do you gain by following him?

THIRTY-FIRST SUNDAY
IN ORDINARY TIME
Commandments

[Replaced by All Souls day, 1997 and 2003 (see page 162);
November 5, 2000]

First Reading: Deuteronomy 6:2–6
The Lord is our God.

It is impossible to overstate the importance of the book of Deuteronomy for the formation of both the Jewish and Christian faiths. Portions of the so-called "second law" (Greek: *deuteronomion*) appear to have been written during the time of the reformer King Josiah in Judah, at least fifty years before that kingdom's final collapse. During and after the exile, these fragments were blended with others to create the work we know today. The book narrates an extended moment of great drama. At the end of forty years' wandering in the desert, Israel stands ready to occupy the land promised to them. Through a series of sermons and responses, Moses gives them the Law that will govern their lives. As history has shown, this Law is vital for Jews. It also interprets and purifies existing tradition, thus establishing a pattern followed by early Christian writers, especially Paul and the four evangelists.

This text includes the *Shema,* the call to prayer which Jews have recited twice daily through history: "Hear O Israel! The Lord is our God, the Lord alone!" After commenting on the marvel that the people have lived after hearing God speak to them, Moses accentuates the great commandment: "Fear the Lord your God, and keep all the laws I give you, so you may live. Hear, O Israel, and obey, so that you may grow and prosper in the land flowing with milk and honey. The Lord is our God. Love the Lord alone, with all your heart and your soul and your strength."

Responsorial Psalm: Psalm 18:2–3, 3–4, 47, 51

Second Reading: Hebrews 7:23–28
Jesus…has a priesthood which does not pass away.

Still on the theme of priesthood, the author contrasts Jesus with the priests of the "old covenant." Jesus remains forever. He is therefore always able to save those who approach God through him. Unlike other high priests, Jesus need not sacrifice daily. He has given sacrifice once and for all, when offering himself. The law has established priests, but the word of the oath that came after the law, the "new covenant," appoints Jesus as priest, perfect forever.

Gospel: Mark 12:28–34
You are not far from the reign of God.

After his richly symbolic entry into Jerusalem, Jesus headquarters with the disciples in nearby Bethany. Visiting the city again, he evicts merchants from the temple, and immediately incurs the murderous wrath of the priests and the scribes. In a third visit he finds his authority questioned by priests, scribes, and elders. Before onlookers, he turns the tables on them. Then he teaches with a parable about tenants in a vineyard that challenges the authorities. Questioned about taxes and the resurrection of the dead, he eludes traps and teaches something new. And in today's verses, a scribe breaks ranks to ask Jesus about the first of all the commandments. It is a question asked of rabbis quite frequently.

In reply, Jesus recites today's first reading. You must love the Lord alone, with all your heart and your soul and your strength. He also adds another quotation from the *Torah:* Love your neighbor as yourself (Leviticus 19:18, seventh Sunday in ordinary time, year A). Unlike similar descriptions of the same encounter (Matthew 22:34–40, thirtieth Sunday in ordinary time, year A; Luke 10:25–28, fifteenth Sunday in ordinary time, year C), Mark's does not explicitly connect the two commandments. Even so, they work together to suggest that all the rest of the Law consists of variations on these themes. The scribe accepts this reply and insists that loving the neighbor is worth more than all burnt offerings and sacrifices. And Jesus informs him that he is not far from the kingdom of God. Note that the kingdom is not something in the future. It is here, now. From this point on, Jesus' challengers remain silent, preferring to execute their fatal plans.

Questions for Reflection

•How do you express our love for God, with all your heart, your soul, and your strength? What does the first reading suggest? What does the Mark text add to it?

•Why must we love neighbors as ourselves? How can you do this?

•What is authentic worship? How does Jesus' encounter with the scribe challenge you to prepare for and to participate in liturgy? How does it affirm and challenge the church's liturgical practice?

THIRTY-SECOND SUNDAY
IN ORDINARY TIME

Giving

[Replaced by the Dedication of St. John Lateran, 1997 and 2003 (see page 164); November 12, 2000]

First Reading: 1 Kings 17:10–16

Do not be afraid.

In battle with the corrupt king Ahab over the soul of Israel, Elijah has promised that the Lord will grip the land in drought (1 Kings 17:1). But the drought affects everyone, including Elijah. When the stream that flows by the prophet's hideout finally dries up, the Lord directs him to Zarephath, where a widow will take him in. Arriving, Elijah finds a poignant scene. The widow is gathering sticks to prepare the last meal for herself and her son. The drought has left her with only a handful of flour and a few drops of oil. Even in these dire straits, at Elijah's request, she agrees to prepare a small cake for him before tending to her needs and those of her son. After that, she assumes, she will die. With the phrase that often accompanies divine action, Elijah tells her "Do not be afraid." And as the prophet promises, the Lord sustains the widow and her son for a year.

Responsorial Psalm: Psalm 146:7, 8–9, 9–10

Second Reading: Hebrews 9:24–28

...he will appear a second time....

Catholics tend to shy away from talk about Christ's second coming, maybe because some very vocal people talk about it too much. They so overemphasize the second coming and the judgment to come at the end of the world that they tend to lose sight of what is most important, the Easter through which Christ has already showered love upon the world. These verses, like the rest of the letter to the Hebrews, tend to correct misunderstandings of widely known aspects of Christian belief. They are as appropriate today as they were in the first century.

The author insists that Christ has entered the heavenly sanctuary, which differs entirely from any built by human hands. We are told that now, in the final age of humanity, Christ has taken away our sins once and for all. He will appear again, not to take away sin, for that has already been done. Instead he will bring salvation to those who eagerly await him. It is clear that we are invited to wait for him.

Gospel: Mark 12:38–44

...she gave from her want....

Teaching in the temple area, Jesus denounces the scribes, who make a grand public show of their religion. They support their life-styles on the contributions of widows and others who can least afford to give. For their hypocrisy, and for the injustices they perpetrate upon others, Jesus insists that the scribes will be punished.

It is risky to say such things on the scribes' own turf, but events immediately fulfill what Jesus has described. Sitting with the disciples across from the treasury, Jesus sees wealthy folks depositing large sums. They draw attention to their entry into the temple precincts, and they make sure everyone can see and hear the size of their gifts to the treasury. Amid all the show-offs, Jesus and company spot a poor widow giving two coins. She does this quietly, perhaps even supposing that her little bit is not enough. But Jesus teaches that she has contributed more than all the others, because, like the widow at Zarephath who tended to Elijah, she has given her livelihood.

On the face of it, this story seems to condemn one sort of practice of religion while endorsing another. While it may do both, its location in Mark's account of the gospel suggests that the story also does more. Soon in the narrative, the same sort of contrast is drawn, but in more dramatic terms. Over against the self-righteousness and hypocrisy of religious leaders who, like these scribes, make a public show of their religion, Jesus offers himself on the cross. The story of the widow's mite is really about the cost of discipleship. Whether in charitable giving or in religious devotion, or in any other manner of service, the disciple is to follow the example of the widow. We must give of our very selves.

Questions for Reflection

•What do you fear? More importantly, what does God seem to call you to do, while your fears inhibit you?

•How do you await Christ's coming? What do you do to keep yourself ready?

•How do you practice your religion? If your family, friends, and acquaintances could not see you any more, how would you change the way you practice?

•What must you do, to give of yourself? What must you change, if anything? What will you continue to do?

THIRTY-THIRD SUNDAY
IN ORDINARY TIME

Permanence

[November 16, 1997; November 19, 2000; November 16, 2003]

First Reading: Daniel 12:1–3

Some shall live forever.

In the three centuries before the birth of Jesus, Palestine was governed by Hellenistic kings. Like many of their predecessors, these foreign potentates tried to force the Jews to accept beliefs and practices that were incompatible with their faith in one, powerful yet invisible God. Many resisted, and the rulers found in Jewish resistance a reason to persecute all of the people.

The book of Daniel is set in this context of oppression. Written in the second century before Christ, these verses are "apocalyptic." Like the rest of the book, they veil the author's protest of the king's actions behind stories of Chaldean cruelty imposed upon Judah centuries earlier. They are like much of the New Testament, including today's text from Mark's account of the gospel. They appear to predict the future, but we must also read them as the author's interpretation of current events.

There will come (that is, there has already come) a time unsurpassed in distress. Your people shall escape: Some have escaped already. Many who have died will rise, to live forever.

This latter statement is an early form of a doctrine of the resurrection. Never a belief held by all Jews, it has become an important part of our Christian belief.

Responsorial Psalm: Psalm 16:5, 8, 9–10, 11

Second Reading: Hebrews 10:11–14, 18

…there is no further offering for sin.

Continuing to correct misunderstandings among what seems to have been an audience of Christians who were Jewish, the author also contrasts Jesus with every other priest known to Jewish history. The day-by-day sacrifices of priests, even of high priests, cannot take away sins. But Jesus sacrificed once for all. Now he waits until his enemies are vanquished. He has forgiven our sins. There is no further offering, for none other is necessary.

Gospel: Mark 13:24–32

...heavens and the earth will pass away, but my words will not.

Like the first reading, these verses, are "apocalyptic." Evoking the great prophets, Jesus teaches Peter, James, John, and Andrew apart from the other disciples. "Look at the signs," he tells them. "Read what history and current events have to tell us. There will be trials of every sort. The sun and the moon and the stars will fall dark. Then people will see the Son of Man coming in the clouds, and he will dispatch his messengers. As the fig tree sprouting leaves heralds the approach of summer, signs will tell you when the Son of Man approaches. [This phrase naming a divine figure comes from Daniel 7:13–14, Christ the King Sunday, year B.] All created things will be destroyed, but my words will endure."

It is hard for us to listen to words like these. They are used often, but rarely with any attention to their real power. Too often, persons with specific political and cultural agenda use these words to judge everyone else. Who has not been accosted by door-to-door salespersons posing as Christians who aim these words as a threat?

But look again at the images connoted in Jesus' words. After all other sources of light have been extinguished, the only source of illumination is the Son of Man, whom, and by whom, people will see. In terrifying narrative form, this image simply asserts a truth: Christ is the light of the world. It is also intentionally urgent, telling us to focus our attention on the light.

At the end of the church year, these verses insist that we think about what really lasts. Our tradition teaches that all of the past two millennia have comprised "the last age." We can see signs of the end, as the blooming fig tree tells us that spring is near. But only the Father knows when the end will really come. In the middle of such uncertainty, only one light penetrates the darkness. Only Jesus can sustain.

Questions for Reflection

• What signs of distress do you see in our world? How do you deal with them?

• What difference does it make to you that your sins are forgiven? How does this truth set you free? How does it oblige you?

• What is permanent? How well do you focus on what is permanent? What transitory things occupy your attention and energy?

• What do you value most? What do your actions and choices reveal about your values? How much do you really value what is permanent?

CHRIST THE KING

A king like no other

[November 23, 1997; November 26, 2000; November 23, 2003]

First Reading: Daniel 7:13–14

...his kingship shall not be destroyed.

These verses from Daniel report a vision of "one like a son of man coming on the clouds of heaven." They follow highly symbolic summaries of the rules of four successive foreign powers that dominated the Jewish people beginning with the fall of Judah in the sixth century before Christ. Each dynasty is compared to a beast, and each is vanquished. Today's text describes the heavenly court that is the source of the only real power in the world. The "son of man" is presented to the "Ancient One," and receives dominion, glory, and kingship. This dominion is to be everlasting, this kingship never to be destroyed.

The "Ancient One" is clearly God, the creator of all things. The "son of man," however, is a more fluid term. In the book of Daniel it can refer to a historical figure as well as to the entire Jewish people. Later, Christian belief has identified Jesus as the son of man.

Responsorial Psalm: Psalm 93:1, 1–2, 5

Second Reading: Revelation 1:5–8

See, he comes amid the clouds!

Like much of the book of Daniel, our book of Revelation is apocalyptic. That is, while its tone and language imply predictions of the future, it also narrates and analyzes history through symbols and images. Here we begin with a profession of faith. Jesus Christ is the faithful witness, ruler of all earthly kings. He loves us and has freed us from sin with his blood. He has made us a royal nation of priests, to serve God. All glory and power are his, forever.

Visionary language portrays him coming amid the clouds. Everyone will see him, even those who have crucified him or otherwise denied him. And all will lament him. That is the way things are, and the way they will be.

Gospel: John 18:33–37

Anyone committed to the truth hears my voice.

These verses are saturated with irony, one of John the evangelist's favorite literary devices. Jesus has been hauled in before Pilate, who demands to know whether he is the king of the Jews. Jesus fires a question right back, effectively placing the Roman governor on trial: "Are you asking on your own, or because of what others say?" Pilate persists, and Jesus makes two main points: first, his kingdom does not belong to this world; second, "king" is Pilate's word, our word, but Jesus has come into the world to testify to the truth. Anyone committed to the truth hears his voice.

In the next verse, not included here, Pilate asks "What is truth?" He cannot recognize the One who is the Truth standing before him. Pilate's failure completes the irony. Represented by Annas the high priest, Jesus' own people have placed him on trial. But standing defenseless before violence inflicted upon him, he asks hard questions: "Why do you accuse me in private, when I have done everything publicly? Why ask me what I said? Ask those who heard me." Annas sends Jesus to the high priest Caiaphas, with what we must presume to be the same result (John 18:19–24). Now, before the secular authority who can rescue or condemn him, Jesus questions Pilate's motives. Do you ask because you seek a king?

After two millennia Jesus' challenge still rings in our ears. After all this time, still we ask who he is. What motivates us to ask? Are we merely curious? Do we feel pressure from someone else to decide what to do about this disturbing person? Are we looking for our Lord?

We must hear him. At the beginning of John's account of his career, he asks us what we seek (1:38). Here, at the end of his career, and after we have seen evidence, he asks what we believe. He asks us to commit ourselves to the truth, to recognize his kingship over all the world.

Questions for Reflection

• What motivates you to approach Jesus? What do you seek? What do you believe?

• What kind of picture does the word "king" create for you?

• What sort of king is Jesus? Why is he the king?

• What is the truth that Pilate cannot see? How does Jesus testify to the truth?

• How do you hear the truth? How do you enact it?

PRESENTATION OF THE LORD
FEBRUARY 2

One of us

[Sunday, 1997 and 2003; Wednesday, 2000]

Before the liturgical reforms of Vatican Council II, this day concluded the Christmas season. Once called the Purification of Mary, the day was renamed to reflect its true character as a feast of the Lord. As in the past, the church continues to begin this celebration with a procession.

First Reading: Malachi 3:1–4

Lo, I am sending my messenger.

Almost nothing is known about the prophet whose six oracles constitute the book of Malachi. It is clear that he or she lived after the Persians had overthrown Babylon and installed a governor in Palestine (1:8), and after those Jews who returned had rebuilt the temple (1:10). Beyond that, we can only guess. We do not even know the prophet's name. The word which we translate as "messenger" is in Hebrew *malaki*. Verse 3:1 could be a pun on the prophet's proper name, or it could speak of him or her only in terms of function, keeping the author anonymous.

Each oracle makes clear that even after the humbling and purifying experience of exile, the people still act in ways that displease the Lord. God will not accept their polluted sacrifices. The ancient covenant that must be renewed is one of good faith, of life and peace, and unity under one father.

This text places us in the middle of the fourth oracle. The audience has wearied the Lord with callous and unjust words and actions (2:17). "I am sending a messenger [*malaki*] to prepare the way for me. The Lord whom you seek will come to the temple. But who can endure this day? He will purify, like refiner's fire or like fuller's lye, so that they will offer proper sacrifice. Then, as long ago, the sacrifice of Judah and Jerusalem will please the Lord."

Responsorial Psalm: Psalm 24:7, 8, 9, 10

Second Reading: Hebrews 2:14–18

...he had to become like us in every way....

These verses suggest the process by which creeds come to be. Writing possibly before the destruction of the temple in Jerusalem in 70, the author warns a Jewish Christian audience against errors of belief. In other words, the author presents doctrine. Although the official and universal creeds would be promulgated three centuries later, here the author demonstrates that at least one article of the creeds is beyond question, early on. Since people are flesh and blood, Jesus had to take on flesh and blood, in order to rob the devil of his power exerted through death, and to free us. Jesus has not come for the sake of angels, but for Abraham's descendants. It was necessary that he become one of us in every way. Through his suffering he has offered help to everyone who is tempted.

Gospel: Luke 2:22–40
...the grace of God was upon him.

The infancy stories in Luke's account of the gospel are rich with allusions to Hebrew tradition. This text portrays Mary and Joseph as devout Jewish parents who take their baby to Jerusalem to consecrate him (see Exodus 13:1–2) and to be purified themselves with the sacrifice of turtledoves (Leviticus 12:2–8). But Luke innovates, too. He omits any mention of the ritual redemption of a month-old baby (Numbers 3:47–48; 18:15–16). In its place, the responses of Simeon and Anna evoke the memory of the legendary priest Samuel, who as an infant was presented in the temple (1 Samuel 1:22–28).

Simeon blesses the child with the prayer known as the *nunc dimittis*: "Now Lord you can dismiss your servant in peace, for I have seen your saving act." And he informs the parents that Jesus will be the downfall and rise of many in Israel. Our encounter with the prophetess Anna is less detailed. She interrupts her constant prayer in the temple to greet the child, and thenceforth to talk about him to everyone who anticipates Jerusalem's liberation.

Like us in all respects, Jesus is also the messenger who appears suddenly in the temple, and who thereby sets free the aged representatives of Jewish tradition and hope. He is a light to the Gentiles, savior of all.

Questions for Reflection
•Who is a messenger of the Lord? What does he or she do? What does the messenger seek to purify?

•What sacrifice is due the Lord? What must we do to offer pleasing sacrifices?

•Why is it essential that Jesus is one of us?

•Whom does Jesus cause to fall? Whom does he raise? Where do you fit?

SS PETER AND PAUL, APOSTLES
JUNE 29

Pillars

[Sunday, 1997 and 2003; Thursday, 2000]

We believe in Jesus Christ with the apostles. Although many people claim to believe in Jesus Christ only, the more honest and realistic way to state our belief is to acknowledge the apostles' contribution. Everything we know and believe concerning Jesus comes to us from the apostles, literally "those who have been sent." They spread Jesus' ministry to the world, in liturgy and service, in the communities they built, and in their teaching. They created the New Testament, the most important source of our knowledge of Jesus. Apart from the apostles we would have nothing upon which to base our Christian faith, and therefore we would have no faith at all. We must acknowledge our unpayable debt to them.

The solemnity of Saints Peter and Paul reminds us of this truth by celebrating the most important apostles. As Acts narrates, these two tower above all others. Peter and Paul have always been commemorated and celebrated together. Today, through them, we acknowledge all the apostles and the essentially apostolic character of our faith.

[Commentary refers to readings for the Mass of the day. Readings for the vigil Mass are Acts 3:1–10; Psalm 19:2–3, 4–5; Galatians 1:11–20; John 21:15–19]

First Reading: Acts 12:1–11
...the Lord has sent his angel....

The Acts of the Apostles is a sequel. It is Luke's gospel of Christ alive in the church, which follows and depends upon Luke's account of the gospel of Jesus Christ. Jesus and church are animated by the Holy Spirit, who is both literary and theological principle of continuity (see Luke 1:35; 1:42; also 1:15; 1:67; Acts 1:3; 1:5; 1:8; 2:4). Angels play important roles in the action in both accounts (Luke 1:11ff., 1:26ff., 2:9, 2:10), and Herod is a major irritant in both (Luke 9:9).

In this text, Herod takes Peter into custody, meaning to put him on trial, possibly to behead him. The church prays on Peter's behalf, and in the night he is freed from his chains and guided from prison unmolested. Out in the open, Peter comes to his senses and recognizes that the Lord has sent an angel to rescue him.

We ought not to mistake Peter for Jesus. As Luke reports, he has corrected forcefully any such confusion (Acts 10:26). On the other hand, he is a symbol for the church, ever dependent upon the Holy Spirit and messengers, and never deterred from his and our appointed task.

Responsorial Psalm: Psalm 34:2–3, 4–5, 6–7, 8–9

Second Reading: 2 Timothy 4:6–8, 17–18
I am already being poured out....

Paul writes from prison: "I am poured out like a libation. I have fought, raced, kept the faith. The Lord will embrace me, for through me God has preached the gospel to all nations. The Lord will keep me safe."

He speaks for himself, for Peter, and for all of us. At the core of our being, we are sent, we are apostles. We must announce good news everywhere and in all circumstances.

Gospel: Matthew 16:13–19
Who do you say that I am?

At Caesarea Philippi, Jesus asks the disciples, "Who do people say that I am?" They answer: "The Baptizer, Elijah, other prophets." Jesus asks: "Who do you say that I am?" Simon calls him Messiah, Son of the Living God. And Jesus replies: "You are blessed, because only my Father can reveal this to you. From now on, you will be called 'Rock' [Peter], and upon this rock I shall build my church. What you declare bound on earth is bound in heaven, and what you declare loosed on earth is loosed in heaven."

Although Peter fails almost immediately after his insight, and later (Matthew 16:21–27, 26:69–75), the first reading portrays the ultimate trajectory of his life. If flawed Peter is a rock at the foundation of the church, each Christian is a stone who helps to build the structure. If Saul, who once persecuted the church, has become our most important theologian, there is hope for us. Imperfect though we may be, we are the church, in whom Jesus has vested enormous power and authority. Sometimes well and sometimes in spite of ourselves, we are an enduring reality who proclaim the kingdom of God.

Questions for Reflection

• What signs illuminate Christ alive in the church? How does the church appear flawed, in your judgment?

• How are you poured out? How does God preach the gospel through you?

• What sort of rock are you? What must you change or improve?

THE TRANSFIGURATION
AUGUST 6
Rising from the dead

[Sunday, 2000; Wednesday, 1997 and 2003]

Although a formal schism between East and West finally split the church in 1054, for many centuries before that year customs and celebrations evolved differently. This feast is of eastern origin. Its date marks the anniversary of the dedication of a church on Mt. Tabor. In the West, however, whose territory did not include the Holy Land, the transfiguration has been celebrated during Lent because the event is linked to Jesus' desert temptations. Over time, the eastern anniversary date has been accepted into the western calendar. Thus we celebrate the transfiguration twice each year: On August 6 and on the second Sunday in Lent.

First Reading: Daniel 7:9–10, 13–14
...his kingship shall not be destroyed.

These verses describe the Ancient One taking his throne of fire, his clothing snow bright, and everything around him dazzling. Thousands minister to him and attend him. Then one like a son of man comes on the clouds of heaven.

Earlier portions of the book of Daniel summarize in symbol the rules of four foreign powers that have dominated the Jewish people since the fall of Judah. Each dynasty is compared to a beast, and each is vanquished. Today's text describes the heavenly court that is the source of the only real power in the world. It is a dazzling spectacle. The "son of man" is presented to the "Ancient One," and receives dominion, glory, and kingship. This dominion is to be everlasting, this kingship never to be destroyed.

Responsorial Psalm: Psalm 97:1–2, 5–6, 9

Second Reading: 2 Peter 1:16–19
...we were eyewitnesses of his sovereign majesty.

In spite of its own claims (1:1; 1:12–15; 3:1), this letter cannot have been written by Peter. For one reason, it presupposes a collection of Christian writings (3:15–16) that did not exist until at least thirty years after Peter's death. For another, it relies heavily on the letter of Jude, but why would Peter ever rewrite the work of another apostle?

Should we then dismiss the author's claim to have witnessed Christ's transfiguration? If we insist on reading every word of the Bible as factual, as we would expect of a twentieth-century scientific report, then we must dismiss it. If, on the other hand, we read this text sensitively and sensibly, we cannot do that.

Many ancient authors wrote under the names of revered authorities. The Jews and eventually the Christians who produced our Bible were no exception. The Psalms are ascribed to David, for example, but it is widely known that he did not compose them all. The book of Wisdom, written about fifty years before the birth of Jesus, claims to be the work of King Solomon, who lived nine centuries earlier. Here, the author only does what comes naturally. To counter accusations of myth-making, and to present universal ("catholic") doctrine in authoritative language, he (or she) appeals to a tradition concerning Peter. "Yes, I saw the Lord transfigured," says the author. "Pay attention therefore to the reliable prophetic message."

Gospel: Mark 9:2–10

This is my Son, my Beloved. Listen to him.

Jesus takes Peter, James, and John to the top of a mountain where before their eyes he is transfigured, that is, changed in form and appearance. In a scene evoking that portrayed in the first reading, his clothes become dazzling white. Elijah and Moses converse with him. Peter wishes to build booths, or tents, for Jesus and these two Hebrew saints, but this does not happen. Instead a cloud overshadows all, and a voice from the cloud teaches: "This is my beloved Son. Listen to him." It is as if the Ancient One receives him. But then looking around, Peter, James, and John see only Jesus.

As the disciples come down from the mountaintop, Jesus tells them not to speak of this event until after he has risen from the dead. And although they do as Jesus asks, they also continue to discuss among themselves what he means by "to rise from the dead."

Questions for Reflection

•How do you envision God?

•How do you deal with the realization that the Bible is not a collection of factual reports?

•What are the various ways in which Jesus appears to you? How do you respond?

•How do you continue to wrestle with his statement about rising from the dead?

ASSUMPTION
AUGUST 15
Power and glory

Like the feasts of the Trinity and Corpus Christi, the Assumption is often called a "doctrinal" feast. It celebrates an aspect of Catholic belief that has been revealed to the church later in history than the creation of the most recently written words in the Bible. The Assumption celebrates the teaching that Mary was assumed directly into heaven.

First Reading: Revelation 11:19, 12:1–6, 10
Now have salvation and power come.

We ought not to read the book of Revelation, also known as the Apocalypse, as a series of predictions, although many people today do just that. Its visions of dragons and armies and cosmic battles are actually complex interpretations of history and belief. Written under Roman rule, it analyzes Roman oppression and persecution of the church through descriptions of Babylon's actions in the past.

Clothed in sun and stars, a woman wails as she labors to give birth. A dragon destroys vast portions of the sky as it approaches her, and stands before her ready to devour the child. But when the child appears, he is taken to God's throne. The woman flees to the desert, and after a battle in which the dragon is destroyed, a voice booms from heaven: "Now have salvation and power come." In the face of terrifying images of power, the baby triumphs. On the occasion of a feast celebrating Mary's assumption, the church leaves no doubt as to the identity of the mother and the child. Christ has turned all of our notions of power upside down.

Responsorial Psalm: Psalm 45:10, 11, 12, 16

Second Reading: 1 Corinthians 15:20–26
Christ must reign....

Adam has brought death into the world, while Christ brings life. Paul creates a parallel that illuminates the significance of Easter. Christ the resurrected one is the firstfruits of those who have fallen asleep. Paul also draws a structured and certain picture of the final judgment. At Christ's coming, all who belong to him will live anew. After destroying all earthly powers, Christ will hand over the kingdom to the Father.

Some people twist this and similar texts into assumptions about "rapture" and a self-righteousness that hardly seems Christian. They prepare for the end in ways that can only be called individualistic, by following strictly a set of rules concerning speech and behavior. These rules are built upon a dishonest selection and interpretation of biblical texts.

The central mistake in this kind of thinking is the role of Christ's second coming. Some people focus upon it so much that they act as though the first coming never happened. They may protest that Easter is very important to them, but their fascination with the end clearly overwhelms everything else. An authentic Christian life recognizes Easter as the turning point of all history. We must interpret everything through this pivotal event, for it is here that history's final chapter has already begun. Easter has offered salvation to all of us, while holding us responsible to one another. We prepare for the final judgment by taking up our crosses and following Christ's example, not by following someone's idea of rules.

Gospel: Luke 1:39–56
My being proclaims the greatness of the Lord.
Filled with the Holy Spirit, Elizabeth recognizes the child in Mary's womb: "Blessed is she who trusted that the Lord's words to her would be fulfilled." And Mary responds with what we now call the *Magnificat*. Rich with allusions to the Hebrew Bible, this poem consists of two parts framed by an introduction and a conclusion. In the first part, Mary sings in gratitude to the Holy One who has done great things for her. In the second part, she cites examples of God's actions on behalf of Israel, elevating the humble and bringing down the mighty. The two parts reinforce and interpret one another. God acts on behalf of the powerless, turning conventional expectations upside down.

Questions for Reflection
•What sense can it make to say that the woman and child are even more powerful than dragons and armies? How can they be more powerful? What does it take for you to believe this truth?

•What are you doing to prepare for the judgment to come? How often do you think about it? How big a role does it play in your everyday conduct?

•How often do you think of Mary? How does she inspire or challenge you?

•How does God act on behalf of the world's lowly? Through whom does God act?

TRIUMPH OF THE CROSS
SEPTEMBER 14

Recovery

[Sunday, 1997 and 2003; Thursday, 2000]

Like the feast of the Transfiguration, this celebration began as the dedication of a church. Constantine's Basilica of the Resurrection was dedicated in Jerusalem on September 13, 335, and the following day was given over to veneration of a relic of Jesus' cross. Thenceforth the relic was venerated every year on September 14. A similar celebration became part of the Roman calendar in the seventh century.

First Reading: Numbers 21:4–9

...he will recover.

Having lost patience during their wanderings, the people complain against God and Moses: "Why did you take us from Egypt? We are disgusted with this food." And in punishment God sends poisonous snakes, who bite and kill many of the people. Then some of the people come to Moses to express their regrets and to ask him to pray for deliverance. Moses does so, and God directs him to fashion a serpent of bronze and to mount it on a pole. Now anyone bitten may look at the bronze representation and recover.

This primitive story, written some three or four centuries after the exodus, may seek to explain a serpent statue in the temple built by Solomon. Along with other things thought incompatible with true worship, the statue was destroyed during the reforms of Hezekiah (2 Kings 18:4). Its very existence suggests an evolution in Hebrew-Jewish doctrine, an evolution that is echoed in Christianity. We do not have to like the story's portrayal of God to appreciate its power. The people owe everything to God. When they lose sight of this truth, they perish. Like our ancestors, we depend utterly upon God, and yet sometimes we forget this truth. To gaze upon our icon, the cross, is to take a step toward recovery.

Responsorial Psalm: Psalm 78:1–2, 34–35, 36–37, 38

Second Reading: Philippians 2:6–11

God highly exalted him.

Christ's complete emptying of himself lies behind any cross we might use to focus our contemplation. These verses are part of an early Christian hymn. Probably sung at liturgies, the hymn proclaims our most basic beliefs. Christ is God's equal, but he emptied himself, having been born in our likeness. As one of us, he accepted everything that came his way, even death on the cross. And because of this obedient death, God has glorified Jesus and directed all creation to worship him.

Paul insists that our attitude must be Christ's. We must empty ourselves, allow ourselves to be humbled, and accept even suffering as we serve our God and the well-being of creatures.

Gospel: John 3:13–17
...so must the Son of Man be lifted up....

Nicodemus has come to speak with Jesus. Jesus insists that to see the kingdom of God, one must be born of water and Spirit. This phrase reflects what John and John's audience practiced: The church baptized persons who had been molded in Christ's image through service and prayer. This text begins in the middle of the conversation with an allusion to today's first reading. As Moses lifted up an image of the serpent that was killing the Israelites in order to heal these who would gaze upon it, the Son of Man must be lifted up to give eternal life to anyone who believes. The Son has not come to condemn, but to save. The light has come into darkness. Anyone who acts in truth comes into the light.

These images tell us to respond to Jesus on many levels at once. Our lives depend on him. We act in truth. We must love the light that illuminates everything we think, say, and do. We must be born of water and Spirit, guided in a community. We must state plainly what our actions tell the world, that we believe in him.

Too often we delude ourselves into merely going through the motions of religious observance. But that is superstition. Let us contemplate the realities that lie behind the cross, and most especially our commitments that it embodies.

Questions for Reflection
• How do you allow yourself to be poisoned? How, and how often, do you forget your utter dependence upon God? How does God invite you to recover?

• How do you act in truth? How do you express your love for the light that illuminates all of our lives?

• What support do you seek in community? How do you contribute to community?

• How do you venerate the cross?

ALL SAINTS
NOVEMBER 1

Here comes everybody

First Reading: Revelation 7:2–4, 9–14

There was a huge crowd which no one could count.

This text speaks of visions. Because of this it might make us uncomfortable; such things are scarcely credible in our skeptical century. Worse, the text seems to portray not only the end of a human life but the end of all human life. Even worse, it insists that there is to be a judgment exercised on the basis of each person's performance in "the trial" (verse 14). Many people today resist the notion of our lives on earth as any form of trial. But as we react to some things that we might not like, let us not lose sight of the profound hopefulness carried through this text. There is room for everyone in God's kingdom.

Having seen several visions, John now looks upon a crowd so vast that no one could count it. The people who make up this crowd have joined with angels and otherworldly creatures to cry out: "Salvation is from our God...and from the Lamb!"

Who are all these people? They are the ones who have washed their robes in the blood of the Lamb. But who are they? They are people from every time and place in history, from every walk of life and from the whole range of races and family and circumstances. They are tall and short, young and old, chubby and slender, and everything in between. What do these people have in common? There are two things, their humanity and their single-hearted commitment to God's will.

Responsorial Psalm: Psalm 24:1–2, 3–4, 5–6

Second Reading: 1 John 3:1–3

Dearly beloved, we are God's children now.

It is God's love, not our actions, that has made us children of God. This is our true identity. What it all means is not yet clear, but eventually God's children will see God and become just like God. Our choices and actions remain important: We must always hope for what is most true to our nature.

Gospel: Matthew 5:1–12

Blest are the single-hearted.

God's kingdom has enough room to include everyone. Imagine a scene on a hillside in ancient Palestine. You are surrounded by people, more people than you can count, and like everyone else, you gaze toward the top of the hill. A fellow named Jesus begins to speak, and you strain to hear. The crowd quiets down, and you listen: "If you know sorrow or hunger or thirst, if you desire peace or holiness or some connection with God, the kingdom of God is yours."

There is room for everyone in this list, which we know as the beatitudes (see also fourth Sunday in ordinary time, year A). We have all known sorrow and pain and need and want. We know what it is to fall short of our goals, to fail, to stand by watching while others succeed. In these very familiar verses Jesus pronounces "blessed" the entire range of human experience. He has made holy the deepest recesses of our hearts, our minds, our souls. Matthew tells us that Jesus blesses us all at the beginning of his teaching career, offering the kingdom to all.

But if the kingdom is offered to all, another question becomes important: What does it take to stay in the kingdom? Jesus offers a clue in the beatitudes: We must live in hope. The rest of the sermon on the mount (Matthew 5–7) expounds on this clue, and the remainder of Matthew's account of the gospel portrays Jesus living the kingdom before our eyes.

This may be the most "catholic" of feasts. It is "for everybody," or as James Joyce noted, "here comes everybody." Today we remember and celebrate the saints who have gone before us, but we also celebrate what is most true to our human nature. We are God's children. We are invited to discover what it is to be God's children, by living a single-hearted commitment to God's will.

Questions for Reflection

•What or who commands your single-hearted attention? How do your actions, your choices, your ways of spending time and money answer this question?

•For what do you hunger or thirst? How do you try to satisfy your hunger or your thirst?

•How often do you act on behalf of peace? What do you do for peace?

•What do you think holiness is? How important is it to you? What do you do for the sake of holiness?

ALL SOULS
NOVEMBER 2
Eternal life

[Sunday, 1997 and 2003; Thursday, 2000]

This is a commemoration of all the faithful who have died. In antiquity a similar celebration was assigned to the Saturday before the beginning of Lent. Monasteries of the tenth century began celebrating the feast of All Souls on November 2, and Rome followed suit four centuries later. Recent thinking connects the autumn harvest with God's harvest of the faithful. Death is a necessary part of any harvest.

[A large number of readings are possible. In most locales, vigil masses will focus on these texts: Daniel 12:1–3; Psalm 23:1–3, 3–4, 5, 6; Romans 8:31–35, 37–39; John 17:24–26. Readings for an evening Mass are likely to be: 2 Maccabees 12:43–46; Psalm 130:1–2, 3–4, 4–6, 7–8; Revelation 14:13; John 14:1–6. Commentary is provided here for the texts to be used at the day's Masses in most places.]

First reading: Wisdom 3:1–9
The souls of the just are in the hand of God....

This text's second word sets this book apart from all of the rest of what we call the Old Testament. It is the Greek *psyche*, which refers to the immortal soul. Its use here reflects the very late date of the book's composition and the author's familiarity with, and adoption of, notions from Greek philosophy. The tendency of modern Bibles to translate the Hebrew word *nepesh* as "soul" only confuses matters, for that reality is mortal and always embodied. This text therefore gives us the Bible's earliest mention of the soul, as we think of it today, and as Christian thought has always held.

God embraces the souls of the just. The foolish had thought the just to be merely dead, but now they are in peace. If they suffered in life, God rewards their souls. It is as if they are gold, having been proven in the furnace, or sacrificial offerings taken directly to God. They will shine. They will judge nations and rule peoples, and the Lord will be their king forever. They will understand truth and live with God in love.

Responsorial Psalm: Psalm 115:5, 6; Psalm 116: 10–11, 15–16

Second Reading: Philippians 3:20–21

We have our citizenship in heaven....

Most of the factions of first-century Judaism disappeared with the destruction of the temple in 70, and the emergence of rabbinic thinking as dominant and normative. As the first reading suggests, some Jewish thinkers had adopted or transformed ideas from Greek philosophy. Others focused Jewish life on the temple, with its elaborate rituals and sacrifices. Still others expressed a militant nationalism, and others were monks. The latter group, the Essenes, left traces of their life and belief on scrolls hidden in caves around the Dead Sea. These scrolls were discovered by accident in the 1940s.

Paul wrote this letter between 54 and 58, when all the factions were yet alive and well. Conversant in Pharisaic (rabbinic) Judaism and in philosophy, he built Christian theology upon a synthesis of the two. This text speaks of eternal citizenship in heaven as something we enter here and now. No matter what our lot, we can and should look forward to what is to come, for Christ will remake us in his image.

Gospel: John 11:17–27

I am the resurrection and the life....

In this portion of the Lazarus story Jesus is led to the burial place. Lazarus' sister Martha reprimands him for his late arrival: "If you had been here, he would not have died." Jesus assures her that her brother will rise again, and she responds that she knows this. Lazarus will rise on the last day. Jesus teaches that he is the resurrection and the life. Whoever believes in him, if dead, shall come to life, and if alive, shall not die. He asks whether Martha believes, and she responds that she does. She calls him Messiah, Son of God, the one who is to come into the world. These texts celebrate the lives of the faithful who have died and express a deep optimism for their destiny.

Questions for Reflection

• For whom do you pray? Who are the faithful departed who have touched your life?

• What do you ask of God? What do you do for God?

• What are doing for your citizenship in heaven?

Dedication of
the Church of St. John Lateran
November 9

The church

[Sunday, 1997 and 2003; Thursday, 2000]

For the first few centuries the church was practically homeless. Evicted from the synagogue and occasionally persecuted by the empire, Christians found stability in their communities, in service and worship, and in their message, which included the holy books. Worship took place in homes, and eventually in public spaces, some built by the church. A new chapter in the church's history began in 324, when, after his conversion, the emperor Constantine gave the Lateran basilica to the bishop of Rome. This was a large meeting hall that was later dedicated to John the Baptizer. The basilica has remained the cathedral church of the bishop of Rome since its dedication.

This occasion is bittersweet. On the one hand it celebrates the church having earned the recognition and approval of the empire, and thus an end to persecution. On the other hand, it is arguable that Roman endorsement has tempted the church to emphasize many wrong things, while neglecting things that matter.

[Many readings are possible for any Mass celebrating the dedication of a church. Commentary is provided for those texts likely to be used in most locales.]

First Reading: Isaiah 56:1, 6–7
Observe what is right, do what is just.

Having been newly restored to their homeland, the people can rebuild the temple. But the prophet reminds them of what matters: Do what is just. The Lord will welcome all righteous foreigners who observe the sabbath and respect the covenant. All may come to the Lord's holy mountain, and their sacrifices will be accepted. God's house will be a house of prayer for all people.

The text reminds us that the church endured persecution and homelessness for three centuries by sticking to the basics. These have nothing to do with buildings. They are the far more durable realities of message, community, worship, and service. The church is about justice and holiness.

Responsorial Psalm: Psalm 84:3, 4, 5–6, 8, 11

Second Reading: Ephesians 2:19–22

You form a building....

Addressing the Gentile Christians at Ephesus, the author captures the most important sense in which the church is a structure. No longer strangers, writes this secretary to the apostle Paul, you are fellow citizens and members of God's household. You are a building set atop the foundation of apostles and prophets, and capped, and thus held together, by Jesus Christ. The whole is built through him, and in him you are being shaped into a dwelling place for God in the Spirit.

Gospel: John 4:19–24

...those who worship him must worship in Spirit and truth.

Here is a portion of the encounter between Jesus and a Samaritan woman at a well. She has toyed with him, but he has broken down all her defenses. He has identified her deepest secrets, and she calls him a prophet. Her ancestors worshiped on Mt. Gerazim in Samaria. That is one of many bones of contention between them and the Jews, their cousins, who insist that worship is centered in Jerusalem. Jesus responds that soon the place where worship occurs will not matter at all. Authentic worshipers will worship the Father in Spirit and in truth. In fact, these realities concern the Father far more than do place and cult.

Taken out of context, these words could seem to grant license for any behavior. But John's terms are not nearly so vague as to permit self-indulgence. Spirit is the Spirit of God, and truth is Jesus. We must worship God in and through Jesus. Moreover, John has created a distinct vocabulary in which Spirit, Jesus, truth, healing (9:1–41), life (11:1–44), justice (2:13–22, 5:1–18), peace and forgiveness (20:19–23), self-sacrifice (15:13), and life in community (14:15–24) are organically connected. You cannot have one without the others. Authentic worship is built upon justice and forgiveness. It emerges from the oneness that is community in his name. It forgives, and it demands that we forgive and build peace.

Questions for Reflection

- Whom do you welcome? Whom do you neglect?
- What part of the building that is the church are you?
- What is authentic worship? How do you do it? How can you improve? How can the entire church improve?

IMMACULATE CONCEPTION
DECEMBER 8
God's promise and our response

Many people assume incorrectly that this feast commemorates Mary's conception of Jesus. Rather, it focuses a full generation earlier in history, celebrating the circumstances of his mother's life. A doctrinal feast, the Immaculate Conception celebrates Mary's first moment of existence, in the womb of her mother, St. Anne. Together with the Assumption (August 15), the solemnity of the Immaculate Conception honors Mary's life as something extraordinary and worth imitating, from beginning to end. Conceived without sin, Mary is the model Christian, the first disciple, the perfect example of someone who has accepted God's will and shown us how to do the same.

First Reading: Genesis 3:9–15, 20
Why did you do such a thing?

The creation stories in the book of Genesis are read in more differing ways than perhaps any other portion of the Bible. These verses from the second creation story seem to favor an understanding of original sin. The man has eaten the forbidden fruit, from the tree of knowledge of good and evil, and of everything in between. The man appears to have caved in to the temptation to seek to know everything, to become like God, or at least "like a god." When God, brokenhearted, confronts the man and the woman, they make matters worse. The man blames the woman for his action, while she blames the serpent. If the first sin is a pride that can lead to idolatry, then the second sin is a refusal to take responsibility. The two sins stand together to portray the role of evil in the human condition. We demand to be our own gods, but we are also eager to blame the nearest scapegoat for anything that goes wrong. Given this sorry state of affairs, maybe it is a miracle that God has commuted our sentence to hard labor. In the end, the man and the woman venture out from the garden that was once their home, to make their living on the land. To be human is to work hard, to seek companionship, and to cope with our ever-present capacity to sin. It is also to seek God among the various things of our lives.

Responsorial Psalm: Psalm 98:1, 2–3, 3–4

Second Reading: Ephesians 1:3–6, 11, 12

God chose us in him....

This text has been used as part of the foundation for the Calvinist doctrine of predestination.The author, probably a disciple of Paul, teaches Gentile Christians at Ephesus, the site of the cult of the goddess Artemis/Diana. They are to be God's adopted children, since God has chosen them before the world began. Having once been pagans, these people are now adopted children.

Gospel: Luke 1:26–38

Blessed are you among women.

It is easy to see why many people are confused about the focus of this feast. This text announces the angel's announcement to Mary that she will bear a son, who will be called the Son of the Most High. Even so, the feast celebrates Mary, her purity, and above all, her faithful response to everything that has been proposed to her.

Mary shows us a right way to walk before God. Her actions contrast greatly with those of the first man and woman. If ever a promise is tough to swallow, Gabriel's words to Mary surely demand faith. This story embraces many themes. One involves Jewish hopes for a messiah, which are, according to Christians, fulfilled in the baby. Another speaks of the power of God, in whose hands the laws of nature are simply the tools of creation. What may be the most important theme is that the faith of a frightened young girl bears earthshaking consequences.

This feast celebrates that human person who, unique among all of us, was favored to carry God inside her body. More importantly, it also invites all of us to walk rightly before God, as she has done.

Questions for Reflection

•How do you rebel against authority? How are you tempted to rebel against God? How do you deal with these temptations? When you fall into them, how do you face the consequences? What excuses do you use, if any?

•When were you most recently aware that you are God's child? How did this awareness impress itself upon you? What traces of paganism continue to affect your behavior? How does God give you hope to avoid them?

•What frightens you? How has God seemed to speak to you, in your fear? How will you respond to your fear?

•What do you have to do to walk rightly before God? What have you already begun to do? What will you do in the very near future?

Appendix

Diving Deeper—An Invitation to a Good Conversation

Suppose you have decided to accept this book's invitation. You are dissatisfied with swimming on the surface of biblical texts. Whether or not you like or agree with my explanations of the readings, you recognize in them the contours of a world that you want to explore in depth.

What do you do now? There are many possibilities: You could attend lectures and workshops, or you could take classes at a local college or university. You might push yourself through a scholarly commentary, page by painstaking page. You might take a correspondence course. You might participate in a forum conducted via computer and modem on an online bulletin board. All of these can be good, or bad.

Whatever path you choose, I encourage you to participate in some form of genuine *conversation* with biblical texts. Let me explain what I mean. I first encountered this way of thinking about biblical interpretation in Bernard Lee's article "Shared Homily: Conversation that Puts Communities At Risk." Distilling the important and difficult work of thinkers like Hans-Georg Gadamer, Paul Ricoeur, Bernard Lonergan, and David Tracy, Lee advocates a simple procedure. It deals with the complications that must arise when relentlessly meaning-making people approach a text from their unique perspectives. It is also the best way I know to make honest interpretations.

Lee's procedure consists of three stages. In a first stage, reading alone, or better, with a group, you declare initial responses to a text. These usually include likes and dislikes, questions and insights, as well as other things. When all the initial responses have been declared, you proceed to a second stage, in which you consider various scholarly commentaries. It is healthy if you can find honest disagreement among scholars. What you are after in this stage is what Lee and others speak of as the "horizon" of the text. Here you are asking questions about the author's historical circumstances, worldview, and intent, about literary devices and textual variants that affect the shape of the text before us, and about the various ways in which the text has already been interpreted, and more.

Having examined the text's horizon in greater or lesser detail, you then proceed to a third phase in which you determine what the text means. You do this by identifying correlations, or intersections, between the text's horizon and your initial impressions. There are three possible kinds of correlations. First, your initial impressions might coincide exactly with, or nestle comfortably inside, the text's horizon. Because the worlds portrayed in the Bible differ so much from our own, however, it is more likely that your initial impression will collide with the text's horizon, that it does not fit. In this instance, you face a choice. A second possible correlation, then, is that you collide with the text and that you choose not to change your mind. There is a disagreement between what you see in the text and in the text's horizon, and you choose to live with this disagreement. You agree to disagree. The third possibility is that you collide with the text but that you accept its challenge. You decide to try to enter into and live in the text's horizon. Clearly, this latter decision is a step in a person's continuing conversion. Maybe you can begin to see why the lectionary is a uniquely powerful instrument for celebrating conversion in the ongoing life of the church, and particularly in the catechumenate.

Notice the role of *voices* in this procedure. In the first stage, you hear your own voice, and the voices of any other people who share with you the task of interpreting. But you do not allow any of these voices to become "the meaning" of the text. At this point you still have a long way to go. You exercise restraint to defer any judgments about meaning until after you have enlarged the conversation. In the second stage, you listen to voices of others who wear the mantles of "expert." Finally, now that you have listened, you can make informed judgments about the meaning or meanings of a text. (A single text may support more than one meaning.)

A good conversation includes a wide variety of voices. All participants listen. They really listen. An interpretation that emerges from a conversation that includes a wide variety of voices is sure to be more adequate than one that comes from a single voice or a narrow band of voices.

Am I suggesting that we determine meaning by majority vote? Wouldn't a procedure like this leave us at the mercy of a loud crackpot or a forceful-if-misguided written commentary? No, I do not advocate either majority rule or a tyranny of the loudest voice. In fact, I am calling for the opposite of the latter. With Bernard Lee and others, I insist that we take care not to exclude differing voices in our conversation. To make sure that all voices contribute to a real conversation, let me suggest these rules, formulated by David Tracy:

- Say only what you mean;
- Say it as accurately as you can;
- Listen to and respect what the other says, however difficult;
- Be willing to correct or defend your opinions if challenged;
- Be willing to argue if necessary, confront if demanded, endure necessary conflict, change your mind if the evidence suggests.

I hope you will keep these thoughts in mind as you look for a way to go more deeply into biblical texts. Listen for a variety of voices in a conversation in which all can be heard with respect. Also, perhaps now you can appreciate why Bernard Lee speaks of "risk" in the title of his article. A genuine conversation is risky. It might require that we change. A conversation with biblical texts places many of our assumptions and habits at risk. But as millions have known, the risks are worthwhile.

Since I do invite you into conversation with texts, I cannot recommend much of what is called "Bible study," as it is manifested in various churches. Too often, such programs offer only a very narrow band of voices or a single voice. They make the mistake of substituting someone's first impressions for a genuine interpretation of a text. Invariably, this is a prescription for mischief.

Ironically, this kind narrowness may occur more often in "non-denominational fellowships" than anywhere else. Here is an example of what I mean: Not long ago I attended the "newcomers night" hosted by the local chapter of a nationally known Bible study program. The welcome seemed genuine enough, but the orientation for newcomers struck me as overly burdened with program rules and demands. Now I do not object to discipline, especially if it seems worthwhile, but on this occasion I grew increasingly uneasy with what seemed to be a literalist and authoritarian approach to the Bible. My unease went crazy during an hour-long lecture about the day's text, which confirmed all my suspicions about the program. It is literalist and authoritarian. Worse, it rejects biblical scholarship. It does not admit ordained ministers into its "fellowship," ostensibly to maintain lay control. In practice, however, this refusal to admit ministers virtually guarantees that the program will continue to be dominated by a single voice, that of a lay preacher who relies upon the program's approved sources, and who refuses to hear voices that might disturb what he happens to find in the Bible.

Do not misunderstand me. I am not condemning everything that goes by the name "Bible study." I do want to illustrate my discomfort with some manifestations of that term that are all too common. I also want to urge you to be careful. The criteria of good conversation should help you in this regard. I am suspicious of anything that does not place you in regular conversation with many different voices surrounding a biblical text. I hope you will exercise a similar suspicion.

For a more in-depth appreciation of what I call "conversation," please consult the following sources:

Dunning, James B. (1993) *Echoing God's Word*. Arlington, VA: The North American Forum on the Catechumenate.

Lee, Bernard (1987) "Shared Homily: Conversation that Puts Communities at Risk." *Alternative Futures for Worship, volume 3: The Eucharist*. Collegeville, MN: Liturgical Press, pp. 157-174.

McBrien, Philip J. (1992) *How to Teach with the Lectionary*. Mystic, CT: Twenty-Third Publications.

McBrien, Philip J. (1992) *How to Teach with the Lectionary: Leaders' Guide*. Mystic, CT: Twenty-Third Publications.

Tracy, David (1984) Chapters 16-18 in R. Grant with D. Tracy *A Short History of the Interpretation of the Bible* (2d ed., rev. and enlarged). Philadelphia: Fortress.

Tracy, David (1987) *Plurality and Ambiguity*. San Francisco: Harper & Row.

Of Related Interest...

Bringing the Word to Life, Year A
Scripture Messages That Change Lives
Michael R. Kent
The readings for every Sunday of the year are covered, with the two-page reflections serving as the foundation for ongoing translation of Scripture to daily life.

ISBN: 0-89622-639-5, 160 pp, $9.95

Bringing the Word to Life, Year B
Michael R. Kent
Michael Kent presents engaging messages for the reflection and inspiration of everyone interested in the Sunday Gospels.

ISBN: 0-89622-691-3, 152 pp, $9.95

Scripture Reflections Day by Day
Rev. Joseph Donders
These Gospel meditations-366 in all-are current, timely, short enough to be read in any free moment and full of meaning and hope.

ISBN: 0-89622-494-5, 384 pp, $9.95

Lightly Goes the Good News
Making the Gospel Your Own Story
This book offers unique and light-hearted insights into the characters and stories of the New Testament.

ISBN: 0-89622-376-0, 144 pp, $7.95

Seek Treasures in Small Fields
Everyday Holiness
Joan Puls
Puls encourages readers to tap into the "treasures" that lie beneath the "small fields" of everyday life circumstances.

ISBN: 0-89622-509-7, 160 pp, $7.95

Available at religious bookstores or from:

TWENTY-THIRD PUBLICATIONS
P.O. Box 180 • Mystic, CT 06355

For a complete list of quality books and videos call:
1 - 8 0 0 - 3 2 1 - 0 4 1 1